Margarethe von Trotta: Interviews

Conversations with Filmmakers Series
Gerald Peary, General Editor

Margarethe von Trotta
INTERVIEWS

Edited by Monika Raesch

University Press of Mississippi / Jackson

www.upress.state.ms.us

The University Press of Mississippi is a member of the Association of American University Presses.

First printing 2018

∞

Library of Congress Cataloging-in-Publication Data

Names: Trotta, Margarethe von author. | Raesch, Monika editor.
Title: Margarethe von Trotta : interviews / edited by Monika Raesch.
Description: Jackson : University Press of Mississippi, 2018. | Series:
  Conversations with filmmakers series | Includes bibliographical references
  and index. | includes filmography. |
Identifiers: LCCN 2017037699 (print) | LCCN 2017042747 (ebook) | ISBN
  9781496815620 (epub single) | ISBN 9781496815637 (epub institutional) |
  ISBN 9781496815644 (pdf single) | ISBN 9781496815651 (pdf institutional)
  | ISBN 9781496815613 (hardback)
Subjects: LCSH: Trotta, Margarethe von—Interviews. | Motion picture
  producers and directors—Germany—Interviews. | BISAC: PERFORMING ARTS /
  Individual Director (see also BIOGRAPHY & AUTOBIOGRAPHY / Entertainment &
  Performing Arts). | PERFORMING ARTS / Film & Video / Direction &
  Production. | BIOGRAPHY & AUTOBIOGRAPHY / Entertainment & Performing Arts.
  | BIOGRAPHY & AUTOBIOGRAPHY / Women.
Classification: LCC PN1998.3.T775 (ebook) | LCC PN1998.3.T775 A3 2018 (print)
  | DDC 791.4302/33092 [B] —dc23
LC record available at https://lccn.loc.gov/2017037699

British Library Cataloging-in-Publication Data available

Contents

Introduction

Excerpt, phone interview, August 18, 2015:

> **Monika Raesch:** Given your history and versatility in the industry, what advice would you give current aspiring filmmakers?
>
> **Margarethe von Trotta:** To try and understand what your own wish is: do you want to be a filmmaker to become popular, to have admirers, to satisfy your own ego? Or do you have something inside of you that you feel really has to be voiced, as otherwise you could not live. *Ask yourself whether filmmaking is an existential question for you.* . . . It is so difficult what you want to do, especially at the beginning, so one thing that makes it easier is if you only have to look inside yourself and not to others.

Interviewing Margarethe von Trotta was a rejuvenating experience for this editor in many ways. For one, von Trotta speaks her mind. What is more, discussing film history with her is a truly in-depth affair, taking into consideration the role of men and women in a society and the historical circumstances (e.g., post World War II) of any given time. You come away having no doubt that for her, filmmaking *is* an existential question, and that she deeply cares about supporting aspiring and new filmmakers along the way.

"Every person is a kaleidoscope—every person is the sum of many different aspects" (phone interview, 2015). Margarethe von Trotta's kaleidoscope encapsulates several themes prominently: sexism, communication, aspirations, and historical biopics. At least one of them surfaces in every interview and in her own work. Von Trotta was born in Berlin in 1942, during World War II. The city experienced significant destruction during the war. Von Trotta spent her childhood growing up post World War II in a city that needed to rebuild, where basic resources such as food, water, and housing could not be taken for granted. She was raised mostly by her mother, who also had to work to provide for the family. Additionally, her family was stateless, meaning without passports. Decades earlier, the von Trotta family had had to leave Russia due to the Revolution and found themselves without country affiliation. Upon birth, Margarethe received a "stateless passport" by the German authorities, which meant that while she was documented, she was without country affiliation. This made traveling across borders in Europe a serious challenge. (This part of von Trotta's life is illuminated in particular in *The Believer*'s interview that is part of this book's collection.) She only received German citizenship upon her first marriage to a German citizen. Arguably, her childhood and teenage experiences as a person who was "tolerated" but without the full rights a German citizen enjoys set her on a path of having to work very hard to achieve goals. As with any person, we are the sum of our experiences.

This book illuminates the many facets that make up the person known as Margarethe von Trotta. The book presents sixteen interviews—mostly from German publications—from the 1980s until 2015 in chronological order. These are augmented by two unpublished speeches von Trotta gave at the University of Duisburg-Essen as part of a guest residency.[1] These afford the reader the opportunity to hear her speak uninterrupted. With the same principle in mind, I edited my most recent interview as little as possible to preserve the original voices of both Margarethe and myself—in this case, two Germans who are speaking in English, but falling back to their native tongue regularly to respectively express detailed nuances that are easiest articulated in the language one knows best. I hope that the final sum of this book resembles a pastiche—that is, a combination of materials from varied sources—of von Trotta's life as seen through her work in the film industry from the 1960s until the mid-2010s.

As rights were not given to publish older interviews in full, an important excerpt is provided in this introduction to hear a younger von Trotta and to enable the reader to experience how her voice evolved over time. The following interview took place in 1973 and also features her second husband, Volker Schlöndorff, who was an integral part to the beginning of her directing career:

Schlöndorff: . . . Someone who watches a movie on TV perceives it in isolation, out of contact with other people. On the contrary, a movie theater provides an opportunity for socializing and broad communication. And we, the young directors, want to actively affect the viewers' consciousness, encourage their collective thinking about themselves and the surrounding world. We want to hear vibrant discussions, contradictions, arguments after movies, so that the viewers develop an efficient [*sic*], active attitude toward life.

von Trotta: Let's take, for example, our movie *A Free Woman* (*Strohfeuer*) . . . We raise the problem of women's emancipation. *Today is the eve of the International Women's Day, the celebration of women's emancipation. But for the larger part of the world, including our country, this problem has not been solved yet.* [. . .]

The inequality of men and women in West Germany begins with the economic inequality. Even now, the average salary of a woman is substantially lower than that of a man. Additionally, Germany, as well as the other Western European countries, forbids abortion. This together creates more than everyday life obstacles. Much more importantly, this develops a certain psychology in women. The women are brought up in the "patriarchal" traditions, and the stress is made on their domestic responsibilities. The bourgeois women, just like my character, most often become obedient daughters of this environment. As a result, they become deeply convinced that their social position is predetermined by their biological structure. They cannot even imagine that their position is historically determined, that they are a product of a purposeful impact of the society on them. They take their position for granted, think of themselves as inferior to the men, and believe that only a man can provide a real support in life. They do not even try to seek support in life through their own intellectual and spiritual opportunities.

S: But let's get back to our movies. Say, we had a chance to show them in Munich—it's a very different case, there is a lot of students and well-educated people there; this is where the social groups are concentrated that do not match the social structure of the rest of the country. But we are dreaming about a broad interaction with the whole country. Only then the cinema fulfills its social function.

vT: For example, we were in an urgent need to analyze our past, our history. The cataclysms that were unleashed in our country at such monstrous, catastrophic scale in the thirties and forties indeed are deeply rooted in our history. It is very important to understand today why it was in Germany that not a single social revolution has been ever fully completed. . . .

(Excerpt from *Iskusstvo Kino*, 1973, translated by Dmitry Zinoviev[2])

Von Trotta began her career in the film industry as an actress—but not because that was her desire—it was the only way she could enter the world of film production in the 1960s. The door to be a female director—her actual goal—did not open until the mid 1970s. Her ambitions in life and desire to reach her goals illuminate the role of sexism and its evolution over the past four decades. Today, von Trotta is an accomplished iconic German female filmmaker.

Perhaps due to having to fight for her dreams for most of her life, she has become an outspoken woman, demonstrating her belief in equality of the sexes. If she feels it is necessary, she will question an interviewer's capabilities. Historically, many of the journalists interviewing her were male, and she did not and still does not have an issue suggesting to them during an interview that they ask sexist questions, as you will discover in this volume of collected interviews.

She also always explicitly states the seemingly abrupt ending to her flourishing, successful acting career: her ambition had always been to be a movie director. While she had to take a detour via acting—she has thirty-two acting credits to her name, ranging from 1966 until 1989—once she was able to co-direct *Die verlorene Ehre der Katharina Blum/The Lost Honor of Katharina Blum* in 1975, only eight more acting performances are part of her resume. Nonetheless, being an actress resulted in being "at the right place at the right time," as she met important directors, including Rainer Werner Fassbinder and Volker Schlöndorff. The latter would provide her with the opportunity to co-direct her first film about the character Katharina Blum. The success of the film changed von Trotta's future in the film industry. Given that von Trotta first worked as an actress, the interviews she was featured in mostly focused on the film and the director, with her providing a quote. Thus, not being able to gain rights for many of these interviews does not take away from this collection. In the later interviews, she and her works are the main focus. As readers will notice, von Trotta does not wish to spend much time speaking about her early career, as she is not passionate about it. It was a means to an end, a means to direct films.

"When my son was little, he said, 'All they [von Trotta and Schlöndorff] ever do is talk about film'" (unnamed interview, Argos Films and ARTE Développement, 2001). One can imagine the private conversations of a husband and wife team who work in the same profession, especially when both partners are passionate about their work. Eventually, von Trotta's second marriage ended in 1991. Arguably, it had a major impact on her filmmaking career, especially as Schlöndorff had supported her directing aspirations.

The Lost Honor of Katharina Blum, now part of The Criterion Collection, is a film deeply embedded in 1970s Germany. A young woman's life comes under investigation by the police and in turn is scrutinized by the tabloid press after she unknowingly spends a night with a suspected terrorist—the film suggests they have a one-night stand. Schlöndorff and von Trotta successfully created a powerful adaptation of Heinrich Böll's novel of the same name, which had been published in 1974. The film stands as a critique of tabloid journalism (so called "Sensationsjournalismus") during the leftist terrorist attacks of the early 1970s. While the film only enjoyed a limited release in the United States and an appearance at the New York Film Festival, it rose to critical acclaim in Germany, winning several national awards, arguably in part due to its timely narrative. Cinema audiences could easily relate to the happenings and their personal reactions, as they related back to recent German boulevard press happenings.

While "hitting home" to German audiences at the time, the film's plot summary suggests how timely the themes of the film still are to this day. The ethical and moral quandaries of all involved still mirror current tactics and reactions by officials, journalists, and the general public in regards to terrorism and people suspected of terrorist actions. Just as novelist Böll—who was awarded the Nobel Prize for Literature in 1972—wrote novels about at-the-time current themes in German society (such as post–World War II German decay, conspicuous economic consumption in the 1960s, and a society's reaction to the threat of terrorism), so does von Trotta study German history and share it with cinema audiences.

She was able to continue work in the directing chair, even by herself. Following three years after her co-directorial debut, *The Second Awakening of Christa Klages* (1978), a film she directs by herself, is released in movie theaters. To help out a financially struggling day care center, three people rob a bank. The aftermath will bring one of the three, Christa, to temporarily live in hiding in Portugal before facing the consequences of her actions when returning to Germany. Arguably, this film established von Trotta as a female filmmaker in her own right, playing at the Berlin International Film Festival and the Chicago International Film Festival. This book's filmography section provides you with an overview of all of von Trotta's works, including her acting credentials, written work, and TV movies.

"I view myself as somewhat of a psychotherapist" (interview with Andre Mueller, 1986). Von Trotta does not necessarily focus on current topics. Instead, each film focuses on one specific time period, in whichever century: *Rosenstrasse* (2003) tackles WWII Germany while *Vision* (2009) centers on nun Hildegard of Bingen's life, who lived 1098–1179. The films expose themes of the past that have remained relevant to the present day and thus relate to current audiences. Never stated explicitly, her films voice messages at a low(er) volume. While the shading may be subtle at times, it has the potential to make it all the more powerful. Applying Linda Seger's use of film adaptation terminology, you will find von Trotta articulating many specific examples of style—"the particular way that a film is executed"; mood—the creation of an emotion; tone—the "attitude" of characters and the audience towards themselves and others; and shading—the volume at which style, mood, and tone is presented—throughout this book (157–59).

Overall, I selected interviews to provide as much breadth of von Trotta's career as possible. Also, I chose texts that augment one another and aimed to avoid content overlap. This, however, was not always possible due to interviews' focus on the same film, such as three interviews related to the release of the 2009 film *Vision*. However, each piece illuminates the work and the filmmaker differently. The most recent interview, conducted specifically for this volume during the summer of 2015, explores two topics that have surfaced in interviews throughout Margarethe von Trotta's career and thus functions as a reflective piece. Specifically, the topic of authorship is explored, which returns us to the matter of labels that von Trotta dislikes so much. She is, however, labeled an auteur and often referenced when a text lists female auteurs of current cinema. The second focus of the interview is "adaptation." The concept and study of adaptation needs to be considered from a variety of perspectives in regards to von Trotta's work, as she has directed some novel-to-film adaptations, but more often has brought the life of real people to the screen, including *Rosa Luxemburg* and *Hannah Arendt*. This type of adaptation always raises questions of faithfulness to actual events that occurred; comparisons between a historical figure's biography and the on-screen character are always drawn by critics, film scholars, and to some extent audience members. It is in particular these kinds of films that open up a filmmaker to negative criticism in a different way than when adapting fictional material, as some interviews in this book illustrate.

"I don't have a role model, nor do I have a favorite song and no favorite painter" (interview with Andre Mueller, 1986). Over the course of a career, a filmmaker becomes known for specific signatures. Von Trotta is an auteur director. Exploring said signatures' evolution over time becomes part of the discussion of the director's discourse. One of Margarethe von Trotta's signatures that I have come across while editing this book is her dislike for labeling artists, raising the question of how one speaks about somebody's work without summary statements. Is this even possible? As already mentioned, in von Trotta's own words, every person can be described as "a kaleidoscope"—every person is the sum of "many different aspects." While in itself a summary statement, its generalness prevents anybody, including her (film) characters, from being turned into one-dimensional cardboard cut-outs and being grouped or stereotyped as "antagonists," "jokesters," etc.

Besides voicing her opinions in a straightforward manner, she tries to prevent stereotyping somebody or narrowing down meaning of a character, which requires precision. This was the reason we regularly resorted to German in the interview I conducted with her: someone's native tongue provides the greatest vocabulary diversity to express one's thoughts and emotions. On the flip side of the refreshingly German-English blend of conversation, I was left with translating our dual language concoction as faithfully as possible into a coherent English interview.

I faced this dilemma with all the interviews of German origin that are part of this volume (and colleagues of mine took on the challenge for French and Russian sources). My goal was to preserve von Trotta's tone—her directness, at times her bluntness, at other times her charming recollections of childhood memories—so that the reader can feel as though they are in the presence of this great filmmaker as much as possible. For this reason, I include footnotes with German original text whenever the English translation could not capture a subtlety of a German word. Readers familiar with the German language still have the benefit of the original undertone that came with the original German word choice. For the same reason, I left grammatical matters and sentence structure untouched when von Trotta spoke in English—anybody who speaks a foreign language finds him- or herself making errors of that kind once in a while. It is part of that person's kaleidoscope.

To read and learn about a filmmaker means to look at primary sources or at as much "raw material" as possible. I hope you enjoy exploring Margarethe von Trotta's desires, goals, development, and works via this selection of interviews.

My gratitude to the following: Dr. Gerald Peary, for giving me the opportunity to edit this volume; the many editors at the University Press of Mississippi who assisted me throughout the creation of this volume; Margarethe von Trotta; Frank Cooper, JD, Dr. Micky Lee, and Dr. Patricia Reeve for their continued support throughout this project; Dmitry Zinoviev and Marjorie Salvodon for translating interviews for this volume; Wolf-Juergen Raesch for not complaining that I added many long distance calls to his phone bill; and Josephine Anes, Grace Bettinson, Nicholas Coronis, Mike DiLoreto, Sarah Griffis, Andrew Hudson, and Emily Thistle, for their clerical support.

MR

Works Cited

Seger, Linda. *The Art of Adaptation: Turning Fact and Fiction into Film*. New York: Holt Paperbacks, 1992.

Notes

1. Von Trotta held the so-called "Mercator-Professur" at the university during the academic year 2013–2014.

2. This interview appeared in *Iskusstwo Kino*, a now closed journal, volume 6 (1973), pp. 148–52.

Chronology

1942   Born February 21, 1942, in Berlin, Germany; mother Elisabeth von Trotta and father Alfred Roloff (a painter). She and her mother relocate to Düsseldorf after World War II.

1960s   For studies, she relocates to Paris and discovers her passion for film.

1964   Marries first husband, with whom she shares a son.

1966   She makes her acting debut in the German TV movie *Das Vergnuegen, anstaendig zu sein*.

1969–70   Works as an actress at the Small Theater (Kleines Theater) in Frankfurt, Germany.

1968   Divorces first husband. (Some sources state the year of divorce as 1970.)

1971   Marries Volker Schlöndorff and is credited as writer alongside husband for the TV movie *Der plötzliche Reichtum der armen Leute von Kombach*.

1975   She co-directs her first feature film, *The Lost Honor of Katharina Blum*, with her husband Volker Schlöndorff. This is also the first feature film for which she receives screenplay writing credit, again alongside Volker Schlöndorff.

1978   She (solo) directs the feature film *The Second Awakening of Christa Klages*.

1980   Jury member at Venice Film Festival.

1981   Directs *Marianne and Julia* and receives international acclaim with the film. She wins the Golden Lion Award at the Venice Film Festival, the first female director since Leni Riefenstahl (*Olympia*, 1938) to do so.

1982   Von Trotta receives the David di Donatello Award for Best Foreign Director for *Marianne and Julia*.

1983   Directs *Sheer Madness*.

1986   Directs *Rosa Luxemburg* and receives a nomination for the Palme d'Or at Cannes Film Festival for the film.

1988   She is nominated for the Palme d'Or at Cannes Film Festival for *Paura e Amore*. From here on onwards, she regularly directs for television, including episodes for TV series as well as made-for-TV movies. Directs the segment "Eva" for the four-part TV series *Felix*.

1989   Receives a Special Film Award at the 40th Anniversary of the Federal Republic of Germany for *Marianne and Julia*. She shares this award with three other filmmakers, notably with director Rainer Werner Fassbinder in whose films she acted early on in her career.

1991   Divorces Volker Schlöndorff.

1990–93   Enjoys two major collaborations with the Italian film industry and directs the feature films *L'Africana* (1990) and *Il lungo silenzio* (1993).

1995   Appointed jury member at Venice Film Festival.

2003   Directs *Rosenstrasse*. At the Venice Film Festival, she is nominated for the Golden Lion Award for *Rosenstrasse* and eventually is awarded the SIGNIS Award and the UNICEF Award for the same film.

2004   She wins the David Award for Best Foreign Film at the David di Donatello Awards for *Rosenstrasse*. She is also honored with a Lifetime Achievement Award for *Rosenstrasse* by the Women Film Critics Circle Awards.

2007   Directs one episode in the acclaimed German TV series *Tatort*.

2009   Directs *Vision* and wins the Silver Medallion Award at the Telluride Film Festival.

2012   Directs *Hannah Arendt*.

2015   Writes and directs *Die abhandene Welt*.

Filmography

Please note that not all films carry an English title.

DAS VERGNÜGEN ANSTÄNDIG ZU SEIN (1966) (TV Movie)
West Germany
Production Company: Bayerischer Rundfunk
Producer: Franz Josef Wild
Director: Hans Lietzau
Screenplay: Luigi Pirandello (play), Georg Richert (translation)
Cinematography: Hans Egon Koch
Editing: unknown
Music: unknown
Cast: Rolf Boysen, Gisela Stein, Lucie Mannheim, **Margarethe von Trotta**
Black and white, 100 minutes

TRÄNEN TROCKNET DER WIND (1967)
West Germany
Production Company: Kerstin-Film
Producer: unknown
Director: Heinz Gerhard Schier
Screenplay: S. Leithen
Cinematography: Armin Müller, Ralph-Joachim Knoess
Editing: unknown
Music: Peter Weiner
Cast: **Margarethe von Trotta**, Günther Becker, Hermann Holve
96 minutes

MY SWEDISH MEATBALL (1969)
Schräge Vögel / Spielst Du mit schrägen Vögeln
West Germany
Production Company: Ehmck-Film GmbH (Gräfelfing)
Distributor: Cinema Service
Producer: Gustav Ehmck

Director: Gustav Ehmck
Screenplay: Günter Seuren
Cinematography: Egon Mann
Editing: Gustav Ehmck
Music: Holger Münzer
Cast: **Margrethe von Trotta**, Jürgen Draeger, Horst Janson
Color, 91 minutes

BRANDSTIFTER (1969) (TV Movie)
West Germany
Production Company: WDR (Westdeutscher Rundfunk)
Producer: Siegfried Schröder
Director: Klaus Lemke
Screenplay: Klaus Lemke
Cinematography: Robert von Ackeren
Editing: Marianne Katsch
Music: Archivaufnahmen (archival recordings)
Cast: **Margarethe von Trotta**, Iris Berben, Veith von Fürstenberg
Color, 64 minutes

BAAL (1969)
West Germany
Production Company: Hallelujah-Film GmbH, Hessischer Rundfunk (HR),
Bayerischer Rundfunk (BR)
Producer: Volker Schlöndorff, Hellmut Haffner, Hans Prescher
Distributor: Weltkino Filmverleih GmbH
Director: Volker Schlöndorff
Screenplay: Volker Schlöndorff
Cinematography: Dietrich Lohmann
Editing: Peter Ettengruber
Music: Klaus Doldinger
Cast: Rainer Werner Fassbinder, Hanna Schygulla, **Margarethe von Trotta**
Color, 88 minutes

GÖTTER DER PEST (1969)
West Germany
Production Company: Antiteater-X-Film GmbH
Producer: Rainer Werner Fassbinder, Michael Fengler
Director: Rainer Werner Fassbinder
Screenplay: Rainer Werner Fassbinder

Cinematography: Dietrich Lohmann
Editing: Rainer Werner Fassbinder
Music: Peer Raben
Cast: Hannah Schygulla, **Margarethe von Trotta**, Harry Baer
Color, 91 minutes

WARUM LÄUFT HERR R. AMOK? (1969)
West Germany
Production Company: Antiteater-X-Film GmbH
Director: Michael Fengler, Rainer Werner Fassbinder
Screenplay: Michael Fengler, Rainer Werner Fassbinder
Cinematography: Dietrich Lohmann
Editing: Rainer Werner Fassbinder, Michael Fengler
Music: Peer Raaben, Joachiim Leder
Cast: Kurt Raab, Lilith Ungerer, **Margarethe von Trotta**
Color, 88 minutes

DRÜCKER (1969/1970)
West Germany
Production Company: Westdeutscher Rundfunk (WDR)
Producer: Harry Schneider
Director: Franz-Josef Spieker
Screenplay: Otto Jägersberg
Cinematography: Robert van Ackeren
Cast: Frithjof Vierock, Carola Rabe, **Margarethe von Trotta**
Color, 70 minutes

INSPEKTOR A.D. KAMINSKI UND DAS HINDERLICHE KIND (1970) (TV film,
part of the TV series *Hauptbahnhof München*)
West Germany
Production Company: Zweites Deutsches Fernsehen (ZDF)
Director: Maximiliane Mainka, Peter Schubert
Editing: Maximiliane Mainka
Cast: Alfred Balthoff, Robert Klupp, **Margarethe von Trotta**
Color

INSPEKTOR A.D. KAMINSKI UND DER GEPRELLTE TÜRKE (1970) (TV film,
part of the TV series *Hauptbahnhof München*)
West Germany
Production Company: Zweites Deutsches Fernsehen (ZDF)

Director: Maximiliane Mainka, Peter Schubert
Editing: Maximiliane Mainka
Cast: **Margarethe von Trotta**
Color

DER AMERIKANISCHE SOLDAT (*The American Soldier*) (1970)
West Germany
Production Company: Antiteater-X-Film GmbH
Producer: Peer Raben
Director: Rainer Werner Fassbinder
Screenplay: Rainer Werner Fassbinder
Cinematography: Dietrich Lohmann
Editing: Thea Eymèsz
Music: Peer Raben
Cast: Karl Scheydt, Elga Sorbas, **Margarethe von Trotta**
Black and white, 80 minutes

DIE KLEINE SCHUBELIK (1970) (episode as part of the TV series *Der Kommissar*)
West Germany
Production Company: Neue Münchner Fernsehproduktion GmbH
Producer: Helmut Ringerlmann
Director: Georg Tressler
Screenplay: Herbert Reinecker
Cinematography: Rolf Kästel
Editing: Werner Preuss
Music: Herbert Jarczyk (title song only)
Cast: Erik Ode, Günther Schramm, **Margarethe von Trotta**
Black and white, 59 minutes

INSPEKTOR A.D. KAMINSKI UND DER LEBENSLANG VERDÄCHTIGE (1970)
(TV film, part of the TV series *Hauptbahnhof München*)
West Germany
Production Company: Zweites Deutsches Fernsehen (ZDF)
Director: Maximiliane Mainka, Peter Schubert
Editing: Maximiliane Mainka
Cast: **Margarethe von Trotta**
Color

DER PLÖTZLICHE REICHTUM DER ARMEN LEUTE VON KOMBACH (1970)
West Germany
Production Company: Hallelujah-Film GmbH, Hessischer Rundfunk (HR)
Producer: Volker Schlöndorff
Director: Volker Schlöndorff
Screenplay: Volker Schlöndorff, **Margarethe von Trotta**
Cinematography: Franz Rath
Editing: Claus von Boro
Music: Klaus Doldinger
Cast: Georg Lehn, Reinhard Hauff, **Margarethe von Trotta**
Black and white, 101 minutes

PAUL ESBECK (1970/1971)
West Germany
Production Company: Südwestfunk (SWF)
Director: Erich Neureuther
Screenplay: Wolfgang Kirchner
Cinematography: Siegfried Blohm, Adalbert, Plica
Cast: Henning Gissel, Robert Klupp, **Margarethe von Trotta**
Color, 80 minutes

BEWARE OF A HOLY WHORE (1970/1971)
Warnung vor einer heiligen Nutte
West Germany
Production Company: Antiteater-X-Film GmbH, Nova International
Producer: Peer Raaben, Peter Berling
Director: Rainer Werner Fassbinder
Screenplay: Rainer Werner Fassbinder
Cinematography: Michael Ballhaus
Editing: Rainer Werner Fassbinder, Thea Eymèsz
Music: Peer Raben, Gaetano Donizetti, Elvis Presley, Ray Charles, Leonard Cohen
Cast: Lou Castel, Eddie Constantine, **Margarethe von Trotta**
Color, 103 minutes

TOD EINES LADENBESITZERS (1971) (episode as part of the TV series *Der Kommissar*)
West Germany
Production Company: Neue Münchner Fernsehproduktion GmbH
Producer: Helmut Ringelmann

Director: Wolfgang Staudte
Screenplay: Herbert Reinecker
Cinematography: Rolf Kästel
Editing: Werner Preuss
Music: Herbert Jarczyk (title song)
Cast: Erik Ode, Günther Schramm, **Margarethe von Trotta**
Black and white, 59 minutes

DIE MORAL DER RUTH HALBFASS (1971/1972)
West Germany
Production Company: Hallelujah-Film GmbH
Producer: Volker Schlöndorff
Director: Volker Schlöndorff
Assistant Director: Margarethe von Trotta, Klaus-Oliver Keil
Screenplay: Volker Schlöndorff, Peter Hamm
Cinematography: Klaus Müller-Laue
Editing: Claus von Boro
Music: Friedirch Meyer
Cast: Senta Berger, Peter Ehrlich, **Margarethe von Trotta**
Color, 94 minutes (1971 version), 89 minutes (1972 version)

ALKOHOLIKER (1971/1972) (TV movie; also known as DER FALL VON
NEBENAN)
West Germany
Production Company: Studio Hamburg Filmproduktion GmbH
Director: Tom Toelle
Cast: **Margarethe von Trotta**, Gerd Baltus, Ruth Maria Kubitschek

STROHFEUER (1972)
West Germany
Production Company: Hallelujah-Film GmbH
Producer: Volker Schlöndorff
Director: Volker Schlöndorff
Screenplay: Volker Schlöndorff, **Margarethe von Trotta**
Cinematography: Sven Nykvist
Editing: Suzanne Baron
Music: Stanley Myers
Cast: **Margarethe von Trotta**, Friedhelm Ptok, Martin Lüttge
Color, 101 minutes

DESASTER (1972/1973)
West Germany
Production Company: Bavaria Atelier GmbH
Producer: Helmut Krapp
Director: Reinhard Hauff
Screenplay: Manfred Grunert
Cinematography: W. P. Hassenstein
Editing: Jean-Claude Piroué
Music: Mike Lewis
Cast: Klaus Löwitsch, Dieter Laser, **Margarethe von Trotta**
Color, 96 minutes

DIE VERRÜCKTE (1973) (TV movie in the series *Ein Fall für Männdli*)
Switzerland, West Germany
Production Company: Intertel AG
Director: Wolf Dietrich
Cast: Ruedi Wlater, Margit Reiner, **Margarethe von Trotta**

SONDERBARE VORFÄLLE IM HAUSE VON PROFESSOR S. (1973) (episode as
part of the TV series *Der Kommissar*)
West Germany
Production Company: Neue Münchner Fernsehproduktion GmbH
Producer: Helmut Ringelmann
Director: Wolfgang Becker
Screenplay: Herbert Reinecker
Cinematography: Rolf Kästel
Editing: Anneliese Artelt
Music: Herbert Jarczyk (title song)
Cast: Erik Ode, Günther Schramm, **Margarethe von Trotta**
Black and white, 59 minutes

WOCHENENDE MIT WALTRAUT (1973) (TV movie, part of the series *Motiv
Liebe*)
West Germany
Production Company: Studio Hamburg Filmproduktion GmbH
Director: Roger Fritz
Cast: Friedrich Schütter, Claudia Buthenuth, **Margarethe von Trotta**

ÜBERNACHTUNG IN TIROL (1973/1974) (TV movie)
West Germany
Production Company: Hallelujah-Film GmbH
Producer: Volker Schlöndorff
Director: Volker Schlöndorff
Screenplay: Peter Hamm, Volker Schlöndorff
Cinematography: Franz Rath
Editing: Suzanne Baron
Music: Stanley Myers
Cast: **Margarethe von Trotta**, Rita Scherrer, Ivry Gitlis
Black and white, 78 minutes

UNE INVITATION À LA CHASSE (also known as EINLADUNG ZUR JAGD)
(1974) (part of the series *Histories insolites / Fantastische Novellen*)
France, West Germany
Production Company: Technisonor, Cosmovision, Taurus Film
Director: Claude Chabrol
Cast: Jean-Louis Maury, **Margarethe von Trotta**, Henri Attal
Color, 52 minutes

GEORGINAS GRÜNDE (also known as LES RAISONS DE GEORGINA)
(1974/1975) (TV movie)
West Germany, France
Production Company: Bavaria Atelier GmbH, Westdeutscher Rundfunk (WDR),
O.R.T.F.
Producer: Werner Kliess
Director: Volker Schlöndorff
Screenplay: Peter Adler
Cinematography: Sven Nykvist
Editing: Hilwa von Molo
Music: Friedrich Meyer
Cast: Edith Clever, Joachim Bissmeier, **Margarethe von Trotta**
Black and white, 63 minutes

DAS ANDECHSER GEFÜHL (1974/1975) (TV movie)
West Germany
Production Company: Bioskop-Film GmbH
Producer: Eberhard Junkersdorf
Director: Herbert Achternbusch
Screenplay: Herbert Achternbusch

Cinematography: Jörg Schmidt-Reitwein
Editing: Karin Fischer
Cast: Herbert Achternbusch, **Margarethe von Trotta**, Barbara Gass
Color, 65 minutes

THE LOST HONOR OF KATHARINA BLUM (1975)
Die verlorene Ehre der Katharina Blum
West Germany
Production Company: Bioskop-Film GmbH, Paramount-Orion Film Production
GmbH, Westdeutscher Rundfunk (WDR)
Producer: Eberhard Junkersdorf
Director: Volker Schlöndorff, **Margarethe von Trotta**
Screenplay: Volker Schlöndorff, **Margarethe von Trotta**
Cinematography: Jost Vacano, Dietrich Lohmann (first four days)
Editing: Peter Przygodda
Music: Hans Werner Henze
Cast: Angela Winkler, Mario Adorf, Dieter Laser
Color, 106 minutes

DIE ATLANTIKSCHWIMMER (1975/1976)
West Germany
Production Company: Herbert Achternbusch Filmproduktion
Producer: Herbert Achternbusch
Director: Herbert Achternbusch
Screenplay: Herbert Achternbusch
Cinematography: Jörg Schmidt-Reitwein
Editing: Karin Fischer
Cast: Heinz Braun, Herbert Achternbusch, **Margarethe von Trotta**
Color, 81 minutes

DER FANGSCHUSS (also known as COUP DE GRÂCE) (1976)
West Germany, France
Production Company: Bioskop-Film GmbH, Hessischer Rundfunk (HR), Argos
Films S.A.
Producer: Eberhard Junkersdorf
Director: Volker Schlöndorff
Screenplay: Geneviève Dormann, **Margarethe von Trotta**, Jutta Brückner
Cinematography: Igor Luther
Editing: Jane Seitz
Music: Stanley Myers

Cast: **Margarethe von Trotta**, Matthias Habisch, Rüdiger Kirschstein
Black and white, 96 minutes

BIERKAMPF (1976/1977)
West Germany
Production Company: Herbert Achternbusch Filmproduktion
Producer: Herbert Achternbusch
Director: Herbert Achternbusch
Screenplay: Herbert Achternbusch
Cinematography: Jörg Schmidt-Reitwein
Editing: Christl Leyrer
Cast: Herbert Achternbusch, Annamirl Bierbichler, **Margarethe von Trotta**
Black and white, 88 minutes

THE SECOND AWAKENING OF CHRISTA KLAGES (1977/1978)
Das zweite Erwachen der Christa Klages
West Germany
Production Company: Bioskop-Film GmbH
Producer: Eberhard Junkersdorf
Director: **Margarethe von Trotta**
Screenplay: **Margarethe von Trotta**, Luisa Francia
Cinematography: Franz Rath
Editing: Annette Dorn
Music: Klaus Doldinger
Cast: Tina Engel, Silvia Reize, Katharina Thalbach
Black and white, 93 minutes

MARGARETHE VON TROTTA. PORTRÄIT EINER REGISSEURIN (1979) (TV
documentary)
West Germany
Production Company: Diorama-Film GmbH
Producer: Katja Raganelli, Konrad Wickler
Director: Katja Raganelli
Screenplay: Katja Raganelli
Cinematography: Konrad Wickler
Editing: Renate Metzner-Wilde, Lisa Kraemer
Cast: **Margarethe von Trotta**
43 minutes

SISTERS, OR THE BALANCE OF HAPPINESS (1979)
Schwestern oder Die Balance des Glücks
West Germany
Production Company: Bioskop-Film GmbH & Co Produktionsteam KG, West-
deutscher Rundfunk (WDR)
Producer: Eberhard Junkersdorf
Director: **Margarethe von Trotta**
Screenplay: **Margarethe von Trotta**
Cinematography: Franz Rath
Editing: Annette Dorn
Music: Konstantin Wecker, Henry Purcell
Cast: Jutta Lampe, Gudrun Gabriel, Jessia Früh
Black and white, 95 minutes

MARIANNE AND JULIANE (1981)
Die bleierne Zeit
West Germany
Production Company: Bioskop-Film GmbH, Sender Freies Berlin (SFB)
Producer: Eberhard Junkersdorf
Director: **Margarethe von Trotta**
Screenplay: **Margarethe von Trotta**
Cinematography: Franz Rath
Editing: Dagmar Hirtz
Music: Nicolas Economou
Cast: Jutta Lampe, Barbara Sukowa, Rüdiger Vogler
Black and white, 107 minutes

CIRCLE OF DECEIT (1981)
Die Fälschung / La Faussaire
West Germany, France
Production Company: Bioskop-Film GmbH, Artemis Filmgesellschaft mbH, Hes-
sischer Rundfunk (HR), Argos Films S.A.
Producer: Eberhard Junkersdorf
Director: Volker Schlöndorff
Screenplay: Jean-Claude Carrière, **Margarethe von Trotta**, Kai Herrmann
Cinematography: Igor Luther
Editing: Suzanne Baron
Music: Maurice Jarre
Cast: Bruno Ganz, Jerzy Skolimowski, Hanna Schygulla
Color, 110 minutes

SHEER MADNESS (1983)
Heller Wahn / L'amie
West Germany, France
Production Company: Westdeutscher Rundfunk (WDR), Bioskop-Film GmbH,
Les Films du Losange
Producer: Eberhard Junkersdorf, Margaret Ménégoz
Director: **Margarethe von Trotta**
Screenplay: **Margarethe von Trotta**
Cinematography: Michael Ballhaus
Editing: Dagmar Hirtz
Music: Nicolas Economou
Cast: Hanna Schygulla, Angela Winkler, Peter Striebeck
Black and white, 105 minutes

UNERREICHBARE NÄHE (1983/1984)
West Germany
Production Company: Westdeutscher Rundfunk (WDR), MFG Film GmbH, Roxy
Film GmbH & Co. KG
Producer: Dagmar Hirtz
Director: Dagmar Hirtz
Screenplay: **Margarethe von Trotta**, Dagmar Hirtz
Cinematography: Dietrich Lohmann
Editing: Dagmar Hirtz
Music: Nicolas Economou
Cast: Kathrin Ackermann, Klaus Grünberg, Grigitte Karner
Color, 93 minutes

BLAUBART (1983/1984)
West Germany, Switzerland
Production Company: Westdeutscher Rundfunk (WDR), Schweizer Fernsehen
für die deutsche und rätoromanische Schweiz (SF DRS)
Producer: Hartwig Schmidt
Director: Krzysztof Zanussi
Screenplay: Krzysztof Zanussi
Cinematography: Slawomir Idziak
Editing: Liesgret Schmitt-Klink
Music: Wojciech Kilar
Cast: Vadim Glowna, Karin Baal, **Margarethe von Trotta**
Color, 95 minutes

EIN FILM AUS GESTEN, BLICKEN, ZWISCHENTÖNEN. MARGARETHE VON
TROTTA ZU IHREM SPIELFIELM 'HELLER WAHN' (1985) (TV movie)
West Germany
Production Company: ARD
Cast: **Margarethe von Trotta**

BEI DER ARBEIT BEOBACHTET. MARGARETHE VON TROTTA (1985/1986)
(TV documentary)
West Germany
Director: Heide Mundzek, Wolfgang Fischer
Cast: **Margarethe von Trotta**

ROSA LUXEMBURG (1985/1986)
West Germany
Production Company: Bioskop-Film GmbH, Pro-ject Filmproduktion im Film-
verlag der Autoren GmbH, Ziegler Film GmbH & Co. KG, Bärenfilm-Produktion
GmbH
Producer: Eberhard Junkersdorf, Regina Ziegler
Director: **Margarethe von Trotta**
Screenplay: **Margarethe von Trotta**
Cinematography: Franz Rath
Editing: Dagmar Hirtz
Music: Nicolas Economou
Cast: Barbara Sukowa, Daniel Olbrychski, Otto Sander
Color, 123 minutes

FELIX. EPISODE 3: EVA (1986)
(Four episodes by different directors)
West Germany
Production Company: Futura Film GmbH & Co. Produktions KG.
Producer: Theo Hinz
Director: **Margarethe von Trotta**
Screenplay: **Margarethe von Trotta**
Cinematography: Franz Rath
Editing: Jane Seitz
Cast: Ulrich Tukur, Eva Mattes, Annette Uhlen
Color, 86 minutes

THREE SISTERS (1987/1988)
Paura e amore / Fürchten und Lieben / Trois soeurs
Italy, West Germany, France
Production Company: Bioskop-Film GmbH, Cinémax-Générale D'Images S.a.r.l.,
Erre Produzioni
Producer: Angelo Rizzoli
Director: **Margarethe von Trotta**
Screenplay: Dacia Maraini, **Margarethe von Trotta**
Cinematography: Giuseppe Lanci
Editing: Enzo Meniconi
Music: Alessandro Marcotulli
Cast: Fanny Ardant, Greta Scacchi, Valeria Golino
Black and white, 113 minutes

L'AFRICANA (1990)
Die Rückkehr / L'Africaine
Italy, Germany, France
Production Company: Scena International S.r.l., Bioskop-Film GmbH, Rachel
Productions
Producer: Augusto Caminito
Director: **Margarethe von Trotta**
Screenplay: **Margarethe von Trotta**
Cinematography: Tonino Delli Colli
Editing: Nino Baragli
Music: Eleni Karaindrou
Cast: Barbara Sukowa, Stefania Sandrelli, Sami Frey
Color, 104 minutes

IL LUNGO SILENZIO (1992/1993)
Zeit des Zorns
Italy, Germany, France
Production Company: Evento Spettacolo, Union PN S.r.l., Bioskop-Film GmbH,
KG Productions
Producer: Felice Laudadio, Evento Spettacola
Director: **Margarethe von Trotta**
Screenplay: Felice Laudadio
Cinematography: Marco Sperduti
Editing: Nino Baragli, Ugo De Rossi
Music: Ennio Morricone
Cast: Carla Gravina, Jacques Perrin, Paolo Graziosi
Color, 92 minutes

DAS VERSPRECHEN (1993/1994)
Les années du mur
Switzerland, France, Germany
Production Company: Bioskop-Film GmbH, J.M.H. Productions, Westdeutscher
Rundfunk (WDR), Odessa Films S.A.
Producer: Eberhard Junkersdorf
Director: **Margarethe von Trotta**
Screenplay: Peter Schneider, **Margarethe von Trotta**
Cinematography: Franz Rath
Editing: Suzanne Baron
Music: Jürgen Knieper
Cast: Meret Becker, Corinna Harfouch, Anian Zollner
Color, 115 minutes

DIE NACHT DER REGISSEURE (1994/1995) (documentary)
Germany
Production Company: Edgar Reitz Filmproduktion, British Film Institute TV
Production, Zweites Deutsches Fernsehen (ZDF), Arte G.E.I.E., Premiere TV
Producer: Robert Busch
Director: Edgar Reitz
Cinematography: Christian Reitz, Peter Petridis, Stefan von Borbély
Editing: Horst Reiter, Michael Tischner, Christian Singer, Uwe Limmeck
Music: Nikos Mamangakis, Aljoscha Zimmermann
Cast: Volker Schlöndorff, Helma Sanders-Brahms, **Margarethe von Trotta**
Color, 87 minutes

DIE NEUGIER IMMER WEITER TREIBEN (1995) (documentary)
Germany
Director: Peter Buchka
Cast: **Margarethe von Trotta**

WINTERKIND (1997)
Germany
Production Company: Colonia Media Filmproduktions GmbH
Producer: Sonja Goslicki
Director: **Margarethe von Trotta**
Screenplay: Nicole Jones, **Margarethe von Trotta**
Cinematography: Jörg Widmer
Editing: Inez Regnier
Music: Norbert J. Schneider

Cast: Joachim Kemmer, Lena Stolze, Susanna Simon
Color, 89 minutes

DUNKLE TAGE (1998/1999) (TV movie)
Germany
Production Company: Colonia Media Filmproduktions GmbH
Producer: Sonja Goslicki
Director: **Margarethe von Trotta**
Screenplay: **Margarethe von Trotta**
Cinematography: Franz Rath
Editing: Corina Dietz
Music: Tom Dokoupil
Cast: Suzanne von Borsody, Stefanie Stappenbeck, Steffen Groth
Color, 88 minutes

MIT FÜNFZIG KÜSSEN MÄNNER ANDERS (1998/1999) (TV movie)
Germany
Production Company: Ziegler Film GmbH & Co. KG
Producer: Regina Ziegler, Josef Göhlen
Director: **Margarethe von Trotta**
Screenplay: Alistair Beaton, Martin Hennig
Cinematography: Stefan Spreer
Editing: Gabriela Grausam
Music: Konstatin Wecker
Cast: Senta Berger, Ulrich Pleitgen, Konstantin Wecker
Color, 87 minutes

JAHRESTAGE (1999/2000) (TV miniseries)
Germany
Production Company: Eikon-West gemeinnützige Gesellschaft für Fernsehen
und Film mbH, Eikon gemeinnützige Gesellschaft für Fernsehen und Film mbH
Producer: Wolfgang Tumler
Director: **Margarethe von Trotta**
Screenplay: Christoph Busch, Peter F. Steinbach
Cinematography: Franz Rath
Editing: Corina Dietz
Music: Norbert J. Schneider
Cast: Suzanne von Borsody, Marie Helen Dehorn, Matthias Habich
Color, 4×95 minutes

ROSENSTRASSE (2002/2003)
Germany, Netherlands
Production Company: Studio Hamburg Letterbox Filmproduktion GmbH, Tele-München Fernseh GmbH & Co.
Producer: Richard Schöps, Henrik Meyer, Markus Zimmer
Director: **Margarethe von Trotta**
Screenplay: **Margarethe von Trotta**
Cinematography: Franz Rath
Editing: Corina Dietz
Music: Loek Dikker
Cast: Katja Riemann, Maria Schrader, Jürgen Vogel
Color, 135 minutes

DIE ANDERE FRAU (2003) (TV movie)
Germany
Production Company: Cinecentrum Berlin Film- und Fernsehproduktion GmbH
Producer: Dagmar Rosenbauer
Director: **Margarethe von Trotta**
Screenplay: Pamela Katz
Cinematography: Martin Langer
Editing: Corina Dietz
Music: Norbert J. Schneider
Cast: Barbara Sukowa, Barbara Auer, Stefan Kurt
Color, 89 minutes

ICH BIN DIE ANDERE (2005/2006)
Germany
Production Company: Clasart Film- und Fernsehproduktionsgesellschaft mbH
Producer: Markus Zimmer
Director: **Margarethe von Trotta**
Screenplay: Peter Märthesheimer, Pea Fröhlich
Cinematography: Axel Block
Editing: Corina Dietz
Music: Christian Heyne
Cast: Katja Riemann, Armin Mueller-Stahl, Karin Dor
Color, 104 minutes

UNTER UNS (2006/2007) (TV movie)
Germany
Production Company: Hessischer Rundfunk

Director: **Margarethe von Trotta**
Screenplay: Katrin Bühlig
Cinematography: Axel Block
Editing: Elke Herbener
Music: Christian Heyne
Cast: Andrea Sawatzki, Jörg Schüttauf, Peter Lerchbaumer
Color, 89 minutes

ACHTERNBUSCH (2008) (TV documentary)
Germany
Production Company: Tellux-Film GmbH
Producer: Martin Choroba
Director: Andi Niessner
Screenplay: Andi Niessner
Cinematography: Markus Krämer
Editing: Katja Hahn
Cast: **Margarethe von Trotta**
Color, 90 minutes

VISION (2009)
Germany
Production Company: Clasart Film- und Fernsehproduktionsgesellschaft mbH
Producer: Markus Zimmer
Director: **Margarethe von Trotta**
Screenplay: **Margarethe von Trotta**
Cinematography: Axel Block
Editing: Corina Dietz
Music: Christian Heyne
Cast: Barbara Sukowa, Heino Ferch, Hannah Herzsprung
Color, 111 minutes

DIE SCHWESTER (2009/2010) (TV movie)
Germany
Production Company: Hessischer Rundfunk
Director: **Margarethe von Trotta**
Screenplay: Björn Berger
Cinematography: Axel Block
Editing: Silke Franken
Music: Christian Heyne
Cast: Rosemarie Fendel, Cornelia Froboess, Matthias Habich
Color, 90 minutes

HANNAH ARENDT (2011/2012)
Germany, France, Israel
Production Company: Heimatfilm GmbH + Co KG
Producer: Bettina Brokemper, Johannes Rexin
Director: **Margarethe von Trotta**
Screenplay: Pamela Katz, **Margarethe von Trotta**
Cinematography: Caroline Champetier
Editing: Bettina Böhler
Music: André Mergenthaler
Cast: Barbara Sukowa, Axel Milberg, Janet McTeer
Color, 113 minutes

VERBOTENE FILME (2013/2014) (documentary)
Germany
Production Company: Blueprint Film GmbH
Producer: Felix Moeller, Amelie Latscha
Director: Felix Moeller
Screenplay: Felix Moeller
Cinematography: Isabelle Casez, Ludolph Weyer, Aline Laszlo
Editing: Annette Muff
Music: Björn Wiese
Cast: **Margarethe von Trotta**
Color, 98 minutes

DIE ABHANDENE WELT (2014/2015)
Germany
Production Company: Clasart Film- und Fernsehproduktionsgesellschaft mbH
Producer: Markus Zimmer
Director: **Margarethe von Trotta**
Screenplay: **Margarethe von Trotta**
Cinematography: Axel Block
Editor: Bettina Böhler
Music: Scen Rossenbach, Florian van Volxem
Cast: Barbara Sukowa, Katja Riemann, Matthias Habich
Color, 101 minutes

THE ODD COUPLE (2017) (in pre-production)
Germany
Production Company: Heimatfilm
Director: **Margarethe von Trotta**

Screenplay: Pamela Katz
Cast: Katja Riemann, Matthew Sanders

INGMAR BERGMAN—VERMÄCHTNIS EINES JAHRHUNDERTGENIES (2018)
(announced) (documentary)
Germany
Production Company: C-Films
Directors: **Margarethe von Trotta**, Felix Moeller
Writers: **Margarethe von Trotta**, Felix Moeller

Margarethe von Trotta: Interviews

Film: An Interview with Margarethe von Trotta

Gerald Peary / 1984

From *Boston Review,* April 1984. Reprinted by permission of Gerald Peary.

Margarethe von Trotta's *Sheer Madness* was greeted with sheer malice by the West German press when it premiered at the 1983 Berlin Film Festival. The almost all-male critical coterie took exception, in their intemperately harsh reviews, to von Trotta's ungainly gallery of men. Why must they *all* be such wimps, cowards, misogynists, malcontents in von Trotta's women's consciousness tract?

Von Trotta was shaken, understandably, by *Sheer Madness'*s hostile reception in West Germany, her home country. (She lives in Munich with her husband, Volker Schlöndorff, director of *The Tin Drum* and *Swann in Love.*) She had paid her dues, building from *The Lost Honor of Katharina Blum* (with Schlöndorff as co-director in 1977) to the acclaimed *Marianne and Juliane* in 1982.

Von Trotta believed she was working at the peak of her talents making *Sheer Madness*. Her cinematographer was the brilliant Michael Ballhaus, whom John Sayles brought to America for *Baby, It's You*. Her leads were the most charismatic, capable actresses in West Germany: Hanna Schygulla, Fassbinder's siren-in-residence for *The Marriage of Maria Braun* and *Lili Marleen*, and raven-haired Angela Winkler, who starred recently in Andrzej Wajda's *Danton*. And von Trotta's story was an enticing one: *Entre Nous* sidetracked in a Grimm forest, the tale of a dark, mysterious, alluring friendship between a feminist university professor, Olga (Schygulla), and a depressed, introverted, painter-housewife, Ruth (Winkler). As the amity builds, the males around the women are threatened silly and driven crazy. They pout, they plot, they seek revenge. . . .

I caught up with Margarethe von Trotta at the August 1983 Montreal World Film Festival.

While *Sheer Madness* unreeled, von Trotta and I adjourned to a neighboring upscale tavern, filling up quickly for the late afternoon. Among the swinging doctors and lawyers of a Quebecois Happy Hour, we started out talking about the unseemly men who populate *Sheer Madness*. Does von Trotta agree with the film's detractors, that she is "unfair" to men?

"Well, a lot of women have written to me and said that the men in their lives are like that," von Trotta said, beginning to chain-smoke. (As with most well-traveled West German directors, her English between exhalations is near-perfect.) "But you could say it's a cliché. I feel that I'm describing men from the outside because I can't feel their soul. I can't say that I'm really hating men, but things come out unconsciously."

Even sympathetic audiences have been disturbed by von Trotta's portrayal of the husband of the depressive woman, Ruth. At first, he encourages outside friendship for his lonely wife, trying to bring her out of her sadness. Later on he gets terribly jealous and makes sure that Ruth's first art exhibition is cancelled. At one point he tries to strangle Olga, Ruth's only friend.

"I don't think he's a bad man," said von Trotta, defending the husband. "Women's friendship is new. Men aren't used to this kind of behavior. He reacted in a very helpless way. Anyway, I know lots of husbands who act in this way." To prove her point, von Trotta told me (not for publication) the very personal inspiration for the story, and for the near-strangulation. (Her husband, Volker Schlöndorff, was not involved in the macabre incident.)

After we talked for a time, von Trotta admitted that some of her unfocused anger toward male figures began in childhood, in a strained relationship with her father. As with Ruth's in *Sheer Madness*, her problems centered on painting. "My father was a painter who died when I was ten years old," von Trotta recalled. "He tried to make me paint when I was five or six, but I couldn't really design anything at that age. He loved me a lot, but he told me mother, 'She has no talent.'

"When I was fourteen or fifteen, I had a lot of interest in painting. I tried to paint, but I couldn't. So I started studying art history instead, until I found it wasn't creative.

"My father wanted it so much, so I had to show him I was talented. Perhaps my father is the reason I have trouble with male characters.

"But my mother was always a friend to me, and she sacrificed so much for my development. Even if I'd said I want to be an astronaut, she would have supported me. And maybe that's why I trust women so much, and I don't trust men."

Margarethe von Trotta met Volker Schlöndorff in the early 1960s, when she was an actress in very early Fassbinder movies, *Beware the Holy Whore* and *The American Soldier*. "Fassbinder was so insulted when I married Volker that he didn't want to do any pictures with me. He was so possessive. But when I directed my own pictures, he went around saying I was talented. We had a strange relationship."

The three of them collaborated on an obscure screen adaptation of *Baal*, from

Bertolt Brecht's first play, written in a Buchner-influenced expressionist vein. Schlöndorff directed, von Trotta played Sophie, and Fassbinder starred as Brecht's nihilist, bohemian hero. "He was brilliant in it," von Trotta said of Fassbinder, but the film was poorly distributed because of the disapproval of Brecht's widow, Helene Weigel, lording over the Brecht estate from East Berlin. "She was very much against the film. I'm sure Brecht would have been much more open-minded."

Von Trotta coauthored the scripts of many Schlöndorff films, and she starred in several of his best-directed works, including *A Free Woman* (an autobiographical picture about the disintegration of von Trotta's first marriage) and *Coup de Grâce*. "But I became an actress with the idea to become a director. When I began, I had no chance to become a director. I waited for my chance."

In West Germany, where in the 1980s probably more women make feature films than in any other country, there were no role models at all in directing when von Trotta started. Women produced some documentaries in the mid-1970s, but that was all. Instead, von Trotta saw the American independent feature *Wanda*, made by the late Barbara Loden. "She was married to Elia Kazan, a famous director, and that gave me courage. The fact that she was a *woman* got me going." In 1977, von Trotta began directing pictures alone, making *The Second Awakening of Christa Klages*. Three more films followed.

Interestingly, von Trotta's favorite directors, even today, are men: Ingmar Bergman, Carlos Saura, Robert Bresson. "If I speak of influence, then they influence me. I like Saura's mixture of dreams and fantasy. He is always stirring up realities, and going back to the past, and to childhood, what I do in *Marianne and Juliane*. Bresson is less visible in my work. He has a religious seriousness in his films. He speaks about morality but not on a moralistic level. He's a Jansenist, like Pascal. And with my Protestant background, Bresson is more ascetic than I am. But I believe in suffering—a Protestant, a Nordic feeling. Life without suffering is nothing."

Any discussion of von Trotta's oeuvre inevitably leads to Ingmar Bergman, whose Jungian dream states and split-consciousness women are so like her own. Is there a more quintessentially von Trotta picture than Bergman's *Persona*? Curiously, questions about Bergman's influence were the only ones that made von Trotta slightly edgy. She's always asked about Bergman. Always.

"Surely when I was eighteen in Paris and seeing three films a day at the Cinematheque, they influenced me a lot. I say 'influence' because I feel near to his creations, but certainly I don't imitate him." If anything, playwright August Strindberg seems the ultimate inspiration behind both Bergman and von Trotta, not only *A Dream Play*, obviously, but his one-act drama, *The Stronger*. Therein, the woman who never talks proves the powerful one, not the seemingly cocky woman across the table who never shuts up.

In *Sheer Madness*, the passive, depressive Ruth, played by Angela Winkler, turns out to have the most indomitable will in the movie. She can sit in the dark in her apartment for weeks, thinking, thinking. Finally, the outside world, including "strong" feminist Olga, played by Hannah Schygulla, must come to her and pay court, as if she were the queen.

"It's like a blood transfusion," von Trotta explained, echoing the vampiric view of symbiotic human relationships espoused by Strindberg. "The stronger, Hanna, becomes weaker at the end. She's finally alone. But the 'weaker' Angela becomes stronger and stronger by the friendship. Also, Hanna is a kind of vampire too, without knowing it.

"I feel myself split into these two persons, pulled in two directions.

"As with Hanna, there's the rational part: getting money, convincing people I'm powerful enough to do films. I started so old: I was thirty-five. Volker did his first film at twenty-five. I have a sense of urgency. I have a feeling I have so many things ahead of me, such as a film biography of Rosa Luxembourg, the first murder victim of the German predators.

"But I have much more sympathy with losers than winners. I always fear that I'll lose my dreamy, introverted side—attracted to death and suicide—because I must be so sufficient."

Von Trotta recalled her film *Sisters*, in which one sister slaves all day as an executive secretary at the office and the other, unemployed, retreats from the world, dreams weird dreams, and one day kills herself. The two sides of forty-two-year-old Margarethe von Trotta. Even as she strives to become a world-renowned film director, she empathizes with the frail suicide as much—more?—as the woman workaholic.

"In my film, *Sisters*, someone quotes a little sentence from Erich Fromm: 'Not to want success can be a sign of life, not a sign of death.'"

A Conversation with Margarethe von Trotta about Her Latest Film, *Sheer Madness*

Bion Steinborn / 1984

From *Filmfaust: Internationale Zeitschrift*, pp. 35–39. Interview conducted in German in 1984. Translated by Monika Raesch.

Sheer Madness—a brief plot summary: the movie tells the story of a single woman who feels threatened by her environment. She is neurotic in regards to interactions with other people. She attempts suicide when spending time with friends. During the rescue, Olga finds Ruth and saves her life. This experience is the starting point of a friendship between the two.

Ruth's husband informs Olga that Ruth's brother committed suicide and asks for Olga's help with Ruth. It is her brother's suicide that impacts Ruth's life and being in "sheer madness": she sees herself hanging (like a suicide) in her dreams.

These images are soon replaced by those of rescue fantasies that are the result of the women's friendship. Ruth sees her way to freedom in this friendship, while Ruth's husband tries not to lose all authority. He intervenes, supposedly because he cares so much. As a result, the friendship between Ruth and Olga is over and Ruth explains that she no longer wishes to see Olga. In a dream, Ruth kills her husband. This is the ending of the movie, leaving an open ending as to what will happen next.

The movie narrates Ruth's wishes in black and white dream images. She dreams in black and white, Ruth explains. Similarly, Ruth copies paintings by masters of the craft in black and white. This black/white dream world confronts the colored shots of everyday life in which Ruth's relationships (with her husband and friends) are shown.

Filmfaust: Why the title *Sheer Madness*? Most everything runs in a realistic manner in the film.

Margarethe von Trotta: You mean to say that the madness in our relationships has become the norm? The delusional is related to Ruth. It is represented by black/white; as she explains, she views her world like this. All her dreams culminate in one scene when she shoots her husband. The original German title *Heller Wahn* translates as "sheer madness"; it is a slightly modified term from psychology.[1] Psychology differentiates between latent and overt madness. My variation, *Heller Wahn* (*Sheer Madness*) means to me that which is not rooted in the unconscious. On the contrary, it leads to a clear realization kind of mania/madness. Due to the friendship with Olga, Ruth realizes the truth about her life, her relationship with her husband, and her friendship. This realization is communicated in a mania but nonetheless is a realization. The script ended in a psychiatric ward; however, Ruth does not live there as a sick patient but as a woman who has come to terms with herself and has found peace. However, I cut that in the editing room and chose an open ending instead.

F: Especially interesting is the role of the invisible brother in relation to his sister Ruth and vice versa. What is the relationship between the two? And why her brother and not a friend or father? After all, the meaning of the relationship, the sheer madness, is clearly present.

MvT: From a descriptive viewpoint, I imagined Ruth as a woman that I have been friends with for many years. My girlfriend had a brother who committed suicide by hanging himself. For years, whenever the doorbell rang, she believed it would be him. She was disappointed each time a different person was at the door. Eventually, she no longer opened the door. That's part of her [Ruth's] story. I didn't ponder this further; it just ended up in my script. The behavior was connected with that particular character. Of course, I should have realized the origin, but I didn't think about it. In any case, that's why there is no sister or boyfriend [but a brother figure instead]. I also believe that younger sisters admire their older brothers, but never say that out loud. Ruth is hard on herself for never telling him. During the editing process things are often cut that may give more background information, but, on the other hand, I believe that not everything needs to be explained [in a story].

There is another scene that was cut from the movie as I viewed it as too explicit even though it was the hardest scene to realize. It played in a mosque in Egypt. At first, women were not permitted to enter. Eventually we could. Once we had finished shooting and the lights had been removed, our female overseer—in Egypt you always have a censor present—explained that females had touched one another inappropriately in our scenes, which was not true. After a long, tiring back-and-forth conversation, our two actresses had to reenact the scene again for the

Sheik in his office—just as it happened during the middle ages. He decided that it was an innocent scene and gave his permission. In the scene, the women speak about the first time they met and why Ruth ran away. Olga asks Ruth not to go ahead with another suicide attempt. So the theme here was the idea of rescue. I don't know whether you noticed this when watching the film. Ruth wants to be saved, and Olga is a person who likes to save people. The strange desires to be rescued and to want to rescue somebody eventually culminate in a catastrophe. Olga says to Ruth, "I don't want you to run away anymore, because there won't always be someone who will recuse you. It is impossible for me to always be there." Roth promises Olga that she won't make another suicide attempt, to not run away. While Ruth promises, eventually, in their final quarrel, she does run away in panic, and it hurts her to have broken the promise.

F: Is it a feminist viewpoint that a female friendship assists in murdering husbands?

MvT: I don't think you can interpret the film in that manner. Shooting the husband is not an actual killing. Ruth fights back against the force of love and caring—as too much caring can also become a force—as that can't mask one's own desire to take credit for something. Ruth's husband is a sympathetic, loving man. However, he cares too much and is overprotective to the extent that it halts her self-development. She has to free herself from this pressure [that he exerts]. In her imagination, this becomes a murder that's her own madness. By the way, the murder took place in the novel. In retrospect, I considered it too "flat," too direct and one-dimensional [and therefore added the dream layer].

Wim Wenders's film *The State of Things* (*Der Stand der Dinge*, 1982) ends with both producer and director being shot, which happens rather seldom in real life. He [Wenders] uses it as a metaphor. One can hardly interpret it as an invitation to imitate. I don't want to suggest to women that they need to murder their men in order to live. Then I'd have to do that as well. I don't plan on that. [She laughs.]

Ever since women have begun to ponder about themselves, their wishes and desires, new forms of friendship have emerged between them. Those friendships reach a dimension beyond those of male friendships. The type where you met up for a cup of coffee and discussed problems with the kids and family. But one didn't speak about what one wants to accomplish with one's own life.

Since this shift, I have observed many more men who are jealous of this new type of female friendship—the way women interact with one another, and the men are happy about that. But at the same time, they are worried to lose their women and have a divided reaction to the friendships, and some of this occurs on a subconscious level. Suddenly, what they find intellectually correct turns into what threatens their very lives. As a result, they react in an aggressive manner; most of the time they apologize later; but they become just as angry the next time around. That's what I wanted to describe.

F: Is this the message you want to send to the audience?

MvT: I'm skeptical in regards to messages. It's a way of reducing a film to one plane. I never think of a statement or theme when I write; I think about people and their contradictions. You can't condense those into one statement. You have to give interpretive freedom to the audience to discover what is valuable to them in a given film. To want to send a message makes it appear as though I'm the one with the correct answer [as though I am the one with the correct opinion]. I don't know whether I'm right. I see myself as somebody who chronicles [a life] as opposed to judging it.

I think that I show behavioral patterns of people, and, in this film, women who are a new phenomenon in the way I describe them, because the way women currently interact with one another is relatively new.

F: What is the symbolism of the black/white cinematography in this film? Does it represent the inner state of women and that's the reason for the dreamlike representation? Or is it simply a director's stylistic choice?

MvT: These images only relate to Ruth. There are her images. They represent two different areas of her imagination. On one hand, they show her fantasies of a rescue—the recurring moment of meeting Olga for the first time, when Olga saves her for the first time. On the other hand, they represent her self-destructive moments, her deferred attitudes towards suicide. Running away all the way to one's death. She is only able to turn around from these self-destructive thoughts at the very end. She no longer turns her aggression against herself but projects it outward, against her husband. For the first time, she tries to stand up for herself and attempts to fight back.

F: Almost always you use two structures in the plot line of your films. In this movie, flashbacks are used to create prophecies or function as daydreams—why? Do you always aim to add a protagonist's inner thoughts to communicate the nonverbal in a visual format?

MvT: Nobody only is a product of their current living, of their experiences, or of what they recognize as the reality around them. Dreams, daydreams, thoughts at nighttime, memories . . . they all are part of who we are, part of the reality we experience. Life and our idea of what life is. Thank goodness, the film had the budget to illustrate this.

F: Death is the easiest way to close a movie and also the most common in almost all films to "close" a story. You are using the technique in your film, even if only in form of a vision. Did no alternative exist for Ruth?

MvT: Her visions of death are part of her person(ality). She experienced the death of her brother, which torments her and follows her; she has attempted suicide several times; her horror scenarios always entail death; as a result, it is consequential that the film's final sequence entails death.

Of course, one can imagine a different alternative. The movie leaves open how her life continues following the vision of her husband's death. All we as the viewer know is that she has learned to fight back. She has turned her fear of others into the action of fighting back.

F: Ironically, Ruth's husband is a researcher on a peace movement. He ponders life and living, humanity and overcoming obstacles, while Ruth lives through her own war and peace privately. This is a contradiction that clearly illustrates how mind and body are separate entities—the mind has become independent of the body.

MvT: Originally, something like this was supposed to be part of the film *War and Peace*. That is, war and peace in the personal sphere. Fassbinder wanted to do that. The concept existed but he had not turned it into a script. Following his death, Alexander Kluge suggested I shoot this scene. I didn't have time to do so as I was busy with pre-production for this film. I told him that my movie shared the same theme anyway. I still would have done it, had Fassbinder written a script.

F: Your movie makes many implicit connections with the art and culture offerings in our beautiful country, all the way to the explicit statement: "Everybody has a chance with our culture assholes who are in charge."[2] Character Olga replies, "if he serves her"—how is that conversation to be interpreted?

MvT: Just the way it is said. I have had my share of difficulties with the Offices that deal with arts and culture. It took a long time to receive the green light for my film *Die bleierne Zeit*. I didn't cater to their needs and wants and received many rejections as a result. Looking back, I feel that I did cater to the Office simply because the film was successful. That everybody receives a fair chance is a statement often said by those who received their chance. Many only attribute their success to their own genius, not the calculated behavior that permitted them to make it to the current day. I'm no longer sure how I'm to interpret my success. Sometimes I question whether I'm strict enough with myself.

F: Throughout the film, the music has less of a melody during the daydreaming sequences. It sounds more like a calculated noise to create tension—was this your intent?

MvT: I didn't want traditional music for that scene. I wanted something that would irritate, like a noise that drives you crazy. The composer created that piece based on my direction. I find the other music throughout the film very nice and fitting. There are some moments here and there that I'm not fully happy with. But I also couldn't think of anything better. I tried not to use any music in those moments, but that didn't improve matters either. We simply didn't end up finding the perfect musical score.

F: Repeating divination throughout the film puzzled me. It culminates in the moment in which Ruth is being told about the alleged message present in her coffee grounds in Arabic—without translation. One never knows what is being prophesied in any of these scenes. Did you make that decision as a commentary to the profession of divination or to communicate Ruth's helplessness with reality?
MvT: The viewer can imagine what Ruth is being told, especially from the Arabic woman. I want the audience's fantasy to fill that void. Shortly thereafter, Ruth asks her friend to drive with her to the Provence, even though that represents a detour. She wants to present herself to her family. She wants to prove that she no longer hides or runs away, that she is now strong enough to face her family and their quarreling. Olga asks Ruth: "Is this due to what the fortune teller told you?" Ruth's answer is "silence." But she does not say "no."

F: Do you yourself believe in fortune tellers?
MvT: I'm unsure, but would also not like to admit it openly. I'm not totally untouched [by what they say]. My friend Luisa Francia, who co-wrote the script to *Zweites Erwachen* [*Second Awakening*] with me, practices in that area. She reads cards, produces horoscopes, and her predictions are mostly correct. So: I'm not completely a believer, but I'm curious. Curious, not Believer.

F: One last question: is the woman's success or ability to find oneself still dependent on the man's level of resistance?
MvT: At the moment, yes. It doesn't need to stay that way. If you look at society at large—and our society is still controlled by men—you can't claim that society actively aims to assist the role of women. That's just the way it is, for centuries—or even thousands of years, men have been the ones in power, and it is difficult for them to give up or share that power. Perhaps it would be the same the other way around. Women don't get anything served on a platter[3]; we have to fight for everything. Author Bornemann argues in his book *Das Patriarohat* that women do have the power in a matriarchy but—in contrast to men—never use(d) it to repress men. I also don't think that we simply want to flip the power positions; we are not interested in suppressing the men; we just don't want to be suppressed ourselves.

F: Would you label your films as "women films" or as "films made by women"?

MvT: I'd always say these are films made by a woman, but not specifically made for a female audience. Sure, you notice differences in the way women make films and how men do.

F: In your opinion, what are the most obvious and key differences?

MvT: First of all, we don't differentiate between key differences and minor ones, big and small topics, happenings—whether they occur in the private or public spheres. Secondly, we carefully approach people in that we don't assume to know more about the people we describe.[4] We don't own them; we are as insecure as they are. We let contradictions be, and we don't shy away from being open and honest about the contradictions we hold ourselves.

Notes

1. The following discussion of psychology does not translate well from German into English. The English movie title, *Sheer Madness*, must be considered a popular translation as opposed to a translation based on psychological terminology. The term *madness* is used in general and literary discourse, but not in psychological science. The German word *Wahn* plays well with the way von Trotta uses the double meaning of the words in her German interview. Some of this meaning cannot be translated, however, due to the difference between the terms in the two respective cultures and contexts. In psychological science, the labels, categories, or terms utilized are operationalized and therefore far more specific than the term *madness*. Von Trotta suggests that her main character is potentially psychotic (a person who has lost touch with reality) but the reasons for that could be many from a psychological perspective, including but not limited to bipolar disorder and obsessive-compulsive disorder. (However, the terms *latent* and *overt* as used in the interview do apply.)

2. The original German phrase is "Bei unseren Kulturaerschen hat doch jeder seine Chance."

3. The original German phrase is "geschenkt wird uns nichts."

4. It is unclear whether von Trotta refers to characters inspired by real people or people in her life at this moment. As a result, it is also unclear whether she feels that she does not own the characters she invented or does not own the people she used as inspiration for a character, as she does not know everything about them.

Sheer Madness: An Interview with Margarethe von Trotta

Carol Bergman / 1984

From *Cineaste* 13, no. 4 (1984), p. 47. Interview conducted in English in 1984.
Reprinted by permission of *Cineaste Magazine*.

German filmmaker Margarethe von Trotta has been writing and directing her own films since 1977. Born in 1942 in Berlin, she began her career as an actress, appearing on the stage and in films by Fassbinder and her husband, Volker Schlöndorff. She wrote screenplays for three Schlöndorff films (*The Sudden Fortune of the Poor People of Kombach, A Free Woman, Coup de Grâce*) and codirected two others (*A Free Woman* and *The Lost Honor of Katharina Blum*). In 1977, she launched her career as an independent filmmaker with *The Second Awakening of Christa Klages; Sisters, or The Balance of Happiness* (1981) and *Marianne and Juliane* (1982) followed. Her latest film, *Sheer Madness* (1983), opened theatrically in New York this summer. We spoke with Margarethe von Trotta about her latest film and about her personal and political connections to her work.

Cineaste: Three of your four original screenplays feature sisters, or as in the case of *Sheer Madness*, close friends whose sisterly connection is symbolic. Why are you so fascinated by sisters?

Margarethe von Trotta: I had a very close relationship with my mother. I always believed she told me everything because I told her every secret, everything. My mother died just after the shooting of *Sisters*. Six months later I was on a TV program and I spoke about my mother. I revealed the fact that she was forty-two-years-old and unmarried when she had me. Shortly after the program, I received a letter from a woman in Wiesbaden who was given up for adoption just after her birth. Her name was recorded as von Trotta in her birth documents. She is fifteen years older than I am and lives twenty minutes from our mother's grave. We had different fathers but there is no doubt we are sisters.

C: Did you feel upset or excited by the discovery of a sister? It must be a shock when a fantasy is made real.

MvT: I had a breakdown. I think I must have known, unconsciously, all my life that I had a sister. I might have heard my mother talking about it. Children hear and understand so much. In the film *Sisters*, I called the two sisters Maria and Ana. My real sister's second name is Ana and my second name is Maria. I still cannot figure out why my mother never told me. All my relatives have died so there is no one to ask. But I have pieced together some elements of the mystery. My mother was from a noble family and there were severe moral codes at the time. She probably couldn't tell her family that she was pregnant and she couldn't raise her baby because she had no money. It must have been a terrible grief for her.

C: You seem to use the theme of sisterhood in your films as a metaphor for exploring the divided self of modern Germany. In the symbolic system you create, the dark characters with biblical names, such as Miriam in *Sisters* and Ruth in *Sheer Madness*, represent the unconscious, repressed past of Germany. These "Jewish" women are juxtaposed with the Aryan, efficient types such as Olga in *Sheer Madness* and Maria in *Sisters*. Is the symbolism intentional?

MvT: I am not conscious of the symbolism as I am writing, but I know it is there and later I can see that it functions on both a political and personal level. On the personal level, an individual has to be work oriented and acknowledge her dreams and fantasies to be healthy. To have one or the other is imbalanced. Together, Olga and Ruth in *Sheer Madness*, for example, might be able to achieve the balance of happiness. As a nation, Germany has suffered the same fate. It is a byproduct of the hierarchical, patriarchal system based on efficiency, merit, and obedience. The result is a conflict between public and private "self."

C: How did you feel these conflicts as you were growing up in postwar Germany?

MvT: The original title of *Marianne and Juliane* was *Leaden Times*. Growing up in Germany in the fifties was like growing up under a leaden heaven. We felt that there was a past of which we were guilty as a nation but we weren't told about it in school. If you asked questions, you didn't get answers. We all grew up with that burden. Only afterwards, in the sixties, when society was a little more open minded, did we find out our past and what we had done.

C: Does being a woman interfere with your work as a director?

MvT: It took me a longer time to establish myself. All the woman directors in Germany are in their forties and we are still doing small-budget films. I always say a woman director must be a good housewife: do good cooking with very little.

C: Have you had problems getting men to work for you?

vT: Not very often. I work hard to create harmony on the set. It's very important to me. Some men are not used to a woman director, but when they see I'm a hard worker, that's all they care about.

C: How did you make the transition from acting to screenwriting to directing? Was it difficult?

vT: No, not at all. It was a natural development. As an actress you are aware of everything and, of course, I had the advantage of being able to learn technique from Volker.

C: When did you decide to make your own film?

vT: During the shooting of *Katharina Blum*. Volker and I had totally different ideas about how the film should be made. I knew then that I must do my own films, to let things come out of my own person.

C: Have the balances in your marriage to Volker changed since you've become an independent filmmaker?

vT: Our marriage is better. We both have our work and we consult one another but we are not competitors. I was a little difficult to live with because I wanted to do things but I still couldn't do them. I was resentful and frustrated. Now I am much more relaxed.

"I Don't Know Where I'm Headed": A Conversation with Margarethe von Trotta

Andre Mueller / 1986

From *Die Zeit*, July 11, 1986, no. 29. Interview conducted in German in 1986.
Translated by Monika Raesch. Reprinted by permission of Christine Gerstacker.

Andre Mueller: Your film about Rosa Luxemburg is a document of admiration. You said that she is a woman out of your league. Are you that unhappy with yourself?

Margarethe von Trotta: I'm not sure that one can conclude that result from my comment. Do you want to focus this interview on this topic? Rosa Luxemburg was a woman who made some political impact, at least in Germany. I cannot compare myself with her intellectually. I admire her strength, to step forward and out of your own despair become an activist for an entire class of people. She aimed to assist the working class so that they could also turn their dreams and talents into reality.

AM: What talents?

MvT: You need workers' education associations. You read books, watched movies. The desire for cultural activities was amazing. People coped with their financial burdens by seeking intellectual stimulation. I was surprised how the working class could articulate their thoughts in contrast to today's workers.

AM: What do you think are the reasons for this shift?

MvT: Today we are dealing with a type of "non-freedom." I'm referring to the options the media provides us with in our leisure time. People are content being guided. Having money has not resulted in their freedom.

AM: Could a smart woman such as Rosa Luxemburg predict this behavior?

MvT: How would she have been able to do that?

AM: To ponder the reasons for her own unhappiness first.

MvT: She never did that, because she never saw herself as important enough to do so. The energy she needed to fight was fueled by her desperation. She wanted to inspire changes on a larger scope. She was sensitive to the suffering of others.

AM: You are referring to the suffering of the working class?

MvT: Yes, the suffering of the poor.

AM: But she had never experienced that, having grown up as a daughter of a well-off father.

MvT: Not from personal experience, but she knew what being repressed meant due to being a Jew.

AM: She distracted herself from her own suffering.

MvT: Of course. That's a good thing. Should one rather commit suicide, instead of taking action?

AM: No, not that, but does action always have to involve fighting [an opposition]?

MvT: No. One can also write a book. But Rosa was a politician, not an artist. Though her letters demonstrate that she could have become an author as well.

AM: Would you admire her as much if she had become an author?

MvT: Probably not.

AM: You admire, what you yourself are not.

MvT: Of course, that's obvious. If we now realize that I don't love myself, then I will accept that conclusion. It may very well be that a part of my constant work is motivated by self-hatred. I hate myself in regards to many aspects.

AM: Such as?

MvT: I hate that I'm a jealous person.

AM: Do you hate yourself when you are crying?

MvT: Not really. Though I aim to avoid it while making a movie. I know that my colleague Helma Sanders often cries on the set.[1] I don't do that. It wouldn't be beneficial to anybody. What would happen if I showed a weakness?

AM: You would lose power.

MvT: I don't want power.

AM: Then you would not need to be so self-disciplined.

MvT: I view myself as somewhat of a psychotherapist. As somebody who has to exude strength so that others feel comfortable and can work well.

AM: Don't you think that many things would change if, for instance, Helmut Kohl [German chancellor at the time] would cry in front of the House of Parliament [Bundestag]?

MvT: Bahn did that when Willy Brandt "fell."[2]

AM: Yes, but he regretted it later.

MvT: Oh, really!

AM: He said he would have repressed crying if he had known he was being filmed.

MvT: Again, the terrible trait of discipline.

AM: Just like with you.

MvT: Perhaps. I don't want to force anybody to deal with my pain. I hate when people dig around in their own misery. Perhaps I'm similar to Rosa in that regard—I admire her calmness in situations that she knows she can't change. She never complained about her life or world history. Instead, she waited without self-pity/self-destruction for the moment in which the opportunity presented itself that she could take action. She could turn feelings of unsettledness into energy and could turn energy into calmness.

AM: How was she able to do that? Where did she get her strength to accomplish this?

MvT: From her belief that in the end reason is the winner in history.

AM: As we know now, she deceived herself.

MvT: Yes, but the desire for paradise remains. That always comes from within. On one hand, I have the inner desire for self-destruction; on the other hand, I harbor desire for life.

AM: What gives you hope?

MvT: Basically nothing, except perhaps a few women. Since women can bear children, they focus more on life-affirming matters. Women have a higher life expectancy than men.

AM: Alice Schwarzer would now complain that you emphasize the "motherly" aspect of a woman too much.

MvT: It's her right to do so—who cares. She even suggested that I curry favor with men. All that because I didn't critique Rosa who wasn't a feminist. I found that very amusing. Yesterday, men were outraged because I apparently humiliate them. Following the production of my movie *Heller Wahn/Sheer Madness* men wanted to lynch me. Today, people say I try to curry favor.

AM: What is your relationship with the women's movement?

MvT: Very mixed. There are many trains of thought. One emphasizes the presence and embracing of emotions. Another has the ambition to ignore all emotions [. . .].³ I find that ridiculous as it is an imitation of manly behavior. Men have always believed that repressing one's emotions is essential.

AM: You say that you do the same, at least when involved in a film production.

MvT: That's incorrect. I said I don't like to cry openly. That doesn't mean that I don't show emotion. I reveal myself to others via my actions. You have no idea how uncontrolled my revelations are at times. I put a lot of things into my movies unconsciously. People always ask me what messages I want to communicate. But I don't always know that myself. For example, while shooting *Rosa Luxemburg* I constantly listened to Verdi's *Requiem*. My music tape was set to endless repetition. I didn't think about why I was doing that until the moment when I realized that the movie was its own requiem for me. Nobody understood that. I wanted to bring to the forefront the unconscious desperation this woman (Rosa) felt; a kind of desperation that screams for salvation. Accounts state that during the last week of her life she fainted at least four times per day. That proves that she was aware of her lack of power towards the end. With the loss of her faith she collapsed; she was a fragile, often sick person. Only her faith and strange belief in history permitted her to be a functioning person. Her spirit supported her weak body.

AM: You are confusing spirit with faith.

MvT: During the Middle Ages only one word existed for both. Knowledge and faith were not separate terms. Rosa's spirit would believe. Only her body was more truthful than her spirit in the end, by illustrating to her the pointlessness of her fight. At the moment I'm unsure whether we still even have the possibility to overcome our feeling of powerlessness⁴ and turn into a direction of change.

AM: Perhaps admitting our feeling of powerlessness is already the action needed to be taken.

MvT: I don't believe so. Many people felt powerless during those times, for instance, poets. But what did they accomplish?

AM: At least they did not accelerate the stupefaction of society.

MvT: That's not enough for me, even though I respect and admire poets. I'm currently reading Baudelaire. I love Hölderlin.

AM: But you would not call them your role models.

MvT: I don't have a role model, nor do I have a favorite song and no favorite painter. That's also the reason why I never completed the questionnaire the *FAZ* [*Frankfurter Allgemeine Zeitung*, a German newspaper] has sent me ten times already. I don't respond to this type of imbecility. It's asking for absolute truth, concrete answers. As a young girl, I was very interested in art, went to exhibits and concerts. But I had a new favorite artist every other week, exactly the one I newly discovered.

AM: Did you enjoy growing up as a little girl?

MvT: No, as a child I wanted to be a boy. I found it horrible not to have a penis. There were several boys who chased us girls in the streets and peed on us while running. They didn't just do it standing still. I found that incredibly humiliating, as I could not retaliate in the same way. I spent hours in the bathroom trying to pee at such an angle. But it wasn't possible. Sometimes I wonder why I didn't get the idea to grab "the hose" and turn it against the attacker. Perhaps today I would do that. Back then, I ran away screaming.

AM: A psychiatrist would love this topic.

MvT: I once had started an analysis, but the therapist said I should rather communicate my thoughts via my movies. Freud is useless for women. It wasn't just penis envy that I experienced. When a girl wishes to be a boy, the history of boys being viewed as more valuable as girls for thousands of years has a lot to do with that. Dads always wanted sons—class citizens. Looking at the Greeks, all intellectual work was the exclusive domain of the men. A woman was married off when she turned twelve years old, sat at home from then on, with her role being the "wiper for the male sperm."[5] That left a mark on women. I still feel it today. When I try to talk with men, I realize that they don't care to understand my point of view. I enjoy speaking with other women, as I don't feel I'm "running against a wall." I don't want to make the effort to be understood by men anymore. I don't consider that men have interest in understanding me anymore. Of course, he is interested sexually, but he does not want to know about my despair, my vulnerability, everything that makes me a challenging person. When I speak with a man about my despair, he loses all interest in having sex with me.

AM: Does this also apply to your marriage with Volker Schlöndorff?

MvT: I don't want to talk about this publicly. Volker grew up living with his father and two brothers. His mother passed away when he was young. His father was a dictator. As a result, Volker exhibits some behaviors that one can't change easily. Recently, Christa Wolf asked me what still connects me with Volker.

AM: Is it thankfulness?

MvT: It is a form of loyalty, love, of course, as well. I judge him more carefully in some regards as I don't want to hurt him. But rather he should be thanking me for giving him ideas for his work. Eventually it was time to make my own movies, not to prove that I can do that but because I had always wanted to do so. It wasn't easy. The producers from Hessischen Rundfunk couldn't believe it. When I presented them with my screenplay, they asked what I wanted, why I couldn't keep the status quo with my husband directing and me performing the main lead. Volker helped me in that he promised the station to help out should I be unable to deliver.

AM: Do you speak with him about your work?

MvT: Recently not much. He and I don't share the same interest in topics.

AM: In an earlier interview you said that he makes better films than you do.

MvT: Did I say that? My goodness, I say so many things, horrible. But it's true; he makes big commercial films; he also makes the important ones from the viewpoint of art cinema.

AM: Why are you so humble?

MvT: I don't think of myself as humble. I just don't support artists' planned "moments of genius." I don't care how I look in the end. My focus doesn't include that I have to take down other filmmakers as if it were a competition. I don't need an Oscar to know my value of contributions to the industry. Competitive attitude is a manly stance. I don't associate with it. But if a person can only feel content knowing they are better than I am, I can give them that satisfaction.

AM: Even though it's not your honest opinion?

MvT: No, then it would be a lie. I don't appreciate everything Volker produces. He has no clue what passion means. What I admire in him is his technical execution.

AM: Again admiration!

MvT: You think I have a "complex"? Perhaps you are right. Maybe my dad passed that down to me. He was a painter and tried to teach me his trait by forcing me to draw an array of objects that he had arranged in front of me in a complicated way. Because I couldn't succeed, he said that I didn't have any talent. That left a mark on me. On the other hand, I have developed a healthy level of confidence at this point. I consider my work important, and I will not accept or acknowledge that I have any limitations as to my talent. I want to become even more extreme, even when facing the possibility that it kills me.

AM: More extreme in what way?
MvT: I don't know where I am headed.

AM: Hopefully not into suicide.
MvT: You are never fully safe from that. But I would never do it, just considering my child . . . even though I'm rather depressed at the moment. Chernobyl takes all hope away from me; I'm hopeless. Perhaps you will describe me as a hysteric now.

AM: Definitely not!
MvT: It's not really about me anyway. My God, I've lived long enough. It doesn't matter if I get cancer in ten years. But consider the boy. I was shocked when my son said to me, "Mommy, you know, we are the first generation that won't die of natural causes." There's this theory that when the core of a reactor burns, it drills a hole into the earth, and, as a result, causes a chain reaction that may get the entire world to explode. I can't separate myself from that idea. I'm sitting there like a hypnotized bunny waiting for the explosion.

AM: And still you are laughing.
MvT: Of course. It's funny. The very notion that beloved progress that is meant to further the comfortable lifestyles of every single person results in all of us going crazy has a grotesque side.[6] The belief in progress was firmly believed at the start of the twentieth century. Both capitalists and socialists believed in it. You couldn't tell them apart by that viewpoint.

AM: Rosa Luxemburg believed that as well.
MvT: Yes, sure; she totally agreed with the party in this regard.

AM: It doesn't speak of her as being an intellectual person.
MvT: Do you want to reproach that she wasn't a prophet?

AM: Not, but to be admirable?
MvT: What I like about Rosa is that she never reaches a state of lamenting or self-pity. In contrast, I have the tendency to remove myself from the world, physically,

when I am unhappy. I immediately have thoughts of suicide . . . that doesn't help anybody.

AM: Have you ever attempted suicide?

MvT: No, but the feeling is always present. Why else would you make so many movies in which characters ponder the notion of suicide? My very first short story was about a man who constantly thinks about suicide, but never executes it. Until the day when it happens out of the blue, simply because he is on a bridge. I wrote that story as a young girl.

AM: You are that man.

MvT: Of course, that's me. Every time I'm standing on a bridge I experience that moment of fascination in regards to jumping, even when I'm not in a bad place at that point. I want to let myself fall. I would never hang or shoot myself. Those are aggressive forms of suicide that require planning and preparation. I would not be able to do that. I rather envision to jump to my death from a high tower.

AM: Would you leave a good-bye letter?

MvT: I've never thought of that, as I write a lot anyway. One would find my diary. So the motive would be clear. If I commit suicide, a specific happening, such as jealousy, wouldn't motivate it, but it would rather be motivated as the final act of my entire life.

AM: Do you enjoy being interviewed in this manner?

MvT: Usually, yes. But today I would rather remain silent. There are days when one wants to remain silent. I don't see a point in (re)presenting myself (in a specific way). Could we reschedule the interview?

AM: We are almost done.

MvT: But what I've been saying is random prattle[7], helpless remarks. I'm at war with myself. I no longer know what I want, what I should want. I have the feeling to separate myself into molecules that cannot rejoin. Usually I enjoy a bit of self-analysis and critique to find out what I feel and think. I'm like a young pupil that wants to still learn. I desire wisdom. At the moment, that drives me further into despair though.

AM: Of course. Completed thoughts lead to nothing, according to Sartre.

MvT: Does that mean that if one doesn't want to be unhappy, one has to repress?

AM: Yes, or love.

MvT: Okay, I might not be relaxed enough then. Fassbinder once said to me, I shouldn't try to sound intelligent in interviews. I should just sit and be myself. But I'm not radioactive. I have to take action. I can't wait until I radiate what I want to say.

Notes

1. Helma Sander-Brahms (1940–2014) was a German director, screenwriter, and producer. She directed twenty pieces, including TV movies, feature films, and documentaries in the 1970s and 1980s. Both von Trotta and Sanders-Brahms worked on *Felix* (1988), with Sanders-Brahms directing the segment "Er am Ende." (Von Trotta directed the segment "Eva.")

2. Willy Brandt was Chancellor of the Federal Republic of Germany from 1969 to 1974. Von Trotta refers to a certain happening. Which moment she is referencing specifically could not be 100 percent confirmed. However, it is likely that she is referencing the moment when Willy Brandt addressed his party for the last time in 1974. The only person crying was his colleague Egon Bahr (not "Bahn"). News cameras captured the moment.

3. In the original interview, Margarethe von Trotta added "—das ist mir zerbal." As the portion of the sentence cannot be translated due to the inability to translate the word "zerbal," it has been omitted from the main text.

4. Von Trotta uses the word "Ohnmacht."

5. Von Trotta's exact phrase was ". . . der Abputzer fuer das maennliche Sperma."

6. Von Trotta uses the German idiom "in die Luft gehen" to express her opinion.

7. Von Trotta uses the word "Geschwaetz."

A Great Woman Theory of History:
An Interview with Margarethe von Trotta

Karen Jaehne and Lenny Rubenstein / 1987

From *Cineaste* 15, no. 4 (1987), pp. 24–28. Interview conducted in English in 1987.
Reprinted by permission of *Cineaste Magazine*.

No more appropriate director could be found to make a film about Rosa Luxemburg than Margarethe von Trotta, who has consistently delved into the personal motivations behind political acts, as well as the political responses to private experience. Sisterhood has been examined in-depth in von Trotta's films about contemporary women searching for their fair share of a complex world. With her most recent work, von Trotta investigates an even more complex world—Berlin in the early part of the century under the shock waves of the revolutionary fervor and an impending world war. At the center of that political hurricane is Rosa Luxemburg, researched and revitalized in every aspect of her unique position as a woman and an intellectual. In the following interview, Margarethe von Trotta reveals the sense of purpose and keen intellect that set her on the path to Rosa Luxemburg in the 1980s, a time when peace seems as improbable as it did then, and when a woman in a leadership role is likely to be as lonely and thrown back on her own resources as the little heroine of Rosa Luxemburg.

Cineaste: It was widely asserted that Rosa Luxemburg was the project Rainer Werner Fassbinder was working on at the time of his death. Is that the same project that you developed into your film?

Margarethe von Trotta: For many years I had wanted to do a film about Rosa Luxemburg. But I had told myself I must make at least ten pictures before I would have the basic craft and knowledge to approach such a woman in such a time, because I wanted to apply mastery to it. You may remember a scene in *Marianne and Juliane*, where a photo of Rosa Luxemburg hangs above a desk. That was not only deliberate—it indicated my intention to make that film. And I offered the role at that time to Jutta Lampe to make with me some day. I had thought Jutta resembled Rosa with her high forehead; but as fate likes to have it, it turned out to be the other sister, Barbara Sukowa, who would play Rosa.

C: Is your interest in Rosa Luxemburg of a strictly political or feminist origin? All of your films demonstrate a tough feminism against a chaotic political background, it seems.
MvT: In 1968 during the student upheaval in Germany, Rosa Luxemburg was carried as a poster through the demonstrations in Germany, the only woman among Ho Chi Minh, Mao Tse Tung, Marx, Lenin, and so on. Dragged around through the streets that way, this lonely woman struck me as not really suitable for that company. Do you know that portrait of her, with finely chiseled featured and somewhat saddened expression, most unusual and almost emotional? I bought a few of her shorter political essays and the letters, and she fascinated me immediately. On the one hand, in her political works, she had a clear, concrete style with firm beliefs logically argued and progressive and hopeful, but then, in her letters, she is warmhearted, subtle, and almost poetic. These two dimensions on one woman made me want to address her from the very beginning. It was unusual, perhaps, for me at that time to look into a political mind that also expressed itself on clothes, style, music, literature, and a gigantic scope of humanistic problems. She painted, drew; she had plants and studied botany and biology. She had, in short, an intellectual curiosity that sometimes is suspect in the modern world of narrow expertise. But her spectrum of talent beyond politics is what I really wanted to bring out: how a political mind expresses itself not just in writing and at the podium but in the scope of one's whole life.

C: Did you think of her as a "genius"?
MvT: Ach, the concept of "genius" is truly nineteenth century. I simply admired and respected her. She had patience and worked hard for what she knew and believed to be important on any level. That was the beginning, years ago. I had no idea at that time I could ever *direct* a film. It was beyond my reach, really, as a woman then.

C: Do you know how Fassbinder seized upon the idea?
MvT: No, but upon his death there was a script by Peter Mártesheimer [*Maria Braun*, etc.] which Fassbinder usually took and then molded according to his vision of his subject. Fassbinder's producer then offered the project to me, particularly because he thought as a woman, I might have a special insight. At first, the whole situation made me uncomfortable. I hesitated because I had intended Rosa as my tenth film, you see, but friends insisted that I do it and talked me into it. Even

after agreeing, I had to find my own way, because Mártesheimer's script was not how I conceived of either the character or the history. I don't want to go into it, because it was interesting in its own way, but it did not reflect my understanding of Rosa.

C: Were you able to go right into the project?

MvT: No, it's too sensitive and complex. I spent a year and a half in research in East Berlin. The last two volumes of the first that constitute Rosa's letters were not yet out, and I had to sort out of her other work that ever could inform the film narrative. It was massive. In particular, I talked to historians, and Annelies Laschitza was most helpful. She is the author of a book about Rosa and it struck me that when you become so involved with a historical figure, as we both were, you develop a love and understanding for that person as if there were alive and close to you. But I was still awed by the prospect of bringing her life on the screen, and the way Rosa brought me close to Annelies really helped me face the responsibility of doing this king of historical film. So many minuscule problems—those of a filmmaker—stymied her rather often. Questions of a filmmaker are not those of a historian, but we managed to merge our knowledge, even where she thought the matters not exactly weighty. I attended a Rosa Luxemburg symposium in Paris in 1983, but . . .

C: The historical approach with which you began seems to have let you down at some point.

MvT: Well, the academic language is not cinematic, and since I have read her 2,500 letters several times, at least four or five. I was looking for the individual motivation more than her impact on history. I tried to sink myself into her life as if I were faced with playing her role. I was once an actress, you know. After eighteen months of that kind of research, it still took me six months to complete the screenplay—over several drafts.

C: How did you decide which historical figures to include in her biography, since she knew so many prominent figures?

MvT: I was uncomfortable doing a film that would require a historical analysis and unexpurgated authenticity, because that usually turns into an epic, which is not my kind of film. I would just never do that, because I think it is impossible and potentially kitschy. Her private life interested me so much more than her public role, which is of interest to historians primarily, and in the attempt to show how those two aspects were interwoven, I had to bring in a few personalities from the chapter titles of history. But only where they affected Rosa's private life.

C: Did you do independent research then on the other historical figures and their relationship to the same events?

MvT: No, I tried to portray them as Rosa saw them and described them. I made my point of view—and that of the film—Rosa's. Some might argue that Kautsky or Bebel are wrongly represented, so I decided to cling to Rosa's vantage point and not get into historical squabbles. I omitted Lenin, for example, because I find his whole personage as it has traditionally appeared in films simply embarrassing. I had to avoid the recognition factor of such a major "film" figure. As you know, he has been portrayed in hundreds of films.

C: Did you see her personal story as a tragedy? She seems to shatter on her own principles.

MvT: I don't agree. She certainly had a disciplined ethical sense and she was very hard on herself as well as others. It's important to realize that when Rosa rejects her lover Leo Jogiches, it is not because he has been unfaithful to her but that he lied to her. She was utterly fanatic about truthfulness, especially in private affairs. I believe that she believed, on the one hand, in the idea of absolute love—a personal principle—and, on the other hand, the idea of one love between two people remaining steadfast and true all their lives reigned over their society. The combination seems to have held sway over her subsequent life, for she never again asserted the power of total love. In the two volumes of letters written to Leo, you can perceive the development of their relationship on an intellectual level. But she repeatedly asks him to write her something about their personal life or about his feelings for her. That's why I included the scene where he reads to her from her own letters and asks how that could change. She reacts by challenging him with the fact that he never answered those letters with a single personal word. Only work and the Party! But she wanted life and a child.

C: He also denies her that desire when he warns her in the film that a child would make her horrible, just another woman, and that her ideas are her children.

MvT: That's why, ultimately, she left him, for she could show only one side of herself to him, the political, and her life is proof that politics is not enough. That is the deeper cause of their separation. Their friendship and their work kept them together in some form, but what is really amazing in the letters is that Rosa suddenly uses the formal address instead of the familiar "you" (*Sie* rather than *du*) or she finds oddly formalistic ways of stating things, after that point. Then very gradually over the years, she softens again toward him until after her last time in prison. At that point, they have a very deep love and trust again. He was *the* man in her life.

C: The final scene of the film shows Leo looking back as Rosa is led away, and a certain ambiguity in his expression led many to believe that he knew what was about to happen to her. Did you mean to indicate a betrayal on his part?

MvT: For the audience it may be ambivalent, but for me it's not. He watches her go. He knows he'll never see her again. The situation had become so dangerous, and she would not leave Berlin, although in Berlin her life was utterly in peril. *And* he will be killed only two months later. That, too, he could have predicted. If that kind of interpretation applied, I fear the film would be reduced to the cinema of cliché. Leo is never portrayed in the film as a man capable of such betrayal. It would be uncharacteristic—and stupid from a cinematic point of view. That's all.

C: You introduce Rosa's female friends as powerful influences in her life, but also as an ersatz for her lost love. Was that the case?

MvT: Quite so. I also tried to show the complexity with which she tried to replace Leo through her affair with Kostia Zetkin, the son of her friend Clara, and likewise a substitute son for herself, after Leo has rather refused her the right to have children. She finds both son and lover in Kostia, but it seems to be consolation. Rosa was ultimately very lonely in matters of love.

C: In politics, too, she seemed to have been alone as the only woman permitted to cross into the debates and decision-making circles controlled by men. You make that very clear in the dining room sequence, where the men at the table try to invite her to see to women's affairs in the party . . .

MvT: And she tells them that Clara takes care of that! Clara Zetkin actually was responsible for the women's movement within the party, and she published *Die Gleichheit (Equality)*, a social democratic paper for women. Rosa wrote for that paper occasionally, but did not want only to be assigned to that sector of the party. She insisted on being considered on equal footing with the men and was. During my research, I met an elderly man who had known her and her involvement in politics and he maintained that she was the abiding spirit of the party. And she knew it, and exercised it. She had no complexes at all about being a woman among men.

Her friendship with Clara began as a political association. They struggled together within the left wing of the party and later established, together with Karl Liebknecht and Leo Jogiches, the Spartacus League. Out of the political developed an intimacy and trust for a personal friendship, that was, in turn, dealt a death blow by politics. With Lulu or Luise Kautzky, Rosa enjoyed a close personal friendship from the beginning, until Rosa and Karl Kautsky had a falling out over political positions on the Russian Revolution's impact on their movement. Still, that did not mean they stopped seeing each other. Their contact was cooler, strained. After all, Clara Zetkin wrote *Rosa Luxemburg and Karl Liebknecht* in 1919, and Luise published memoirs in 1929 entitled *Rosa Luxemburg*. Among these people, political principles had a priority over their personal lives, because they saw themselves in historical terms.

C: And yet you were more inclined to sift Rosa's life through the exceedingly personal criteria of our modern vision of life rather than apply the historical dimension by which she measured herself.

MvT: I think I did both, but I limited Rosa's historical importance to the weight it had relative to her other values. She was one of the only revolutionaries to experience such an intense life apart from politics. And beyond that, we must remember that a strictly historical perspective would be safer conceived as a documentary. The lessons of Rosa's life are as valuable for the women I personally know as for those who tote up facts and figures. And I hold the view that, when we study historical personalities, private life is as politically important as public life.

C: The Russian revolution seems to have impressed Rosa enormously and provided a model for the politics she wished to follow in Germany.

MvT: At first. But only initially. Her happiness and enthusiasm gave way about a year after the revolution, when she wrote to Lenin to reprimand him for the elitist thinking. Her belief in social democracy was based on a firm belief in "the spontaneity of the masses," by which she meant that when the masses react to political events, they can be trusted. And that they should, in fact, be followed rather than led in another direction by "know-it-alls' (*Besserwisser*).

In 1906, Rosa came back to Germany from Russia—well, Warsaw, which belonged to Czarist Russia—with the opinion that in the interest of Germany democracy, things could definitely be learned from the events taking place in Russia. Simply by thinking through, "What can one learn and apply to Germany?" That's when she discovered that her colleagues within the party did not feel it applied to their situation. They saw themselves as legally established party in the position to evolve into the governing structure. Verbally they were revolutionary, but in their actions quite cautious, due to "evolutionary" thinking.

C: That's where you chose to begin the film. Why?

MvT: I consider the time in her life from the first Russian Revolution, when she returns full of the spirit of change, to the time of the German revolution, which she had truly believed would be a leap forward for the German people, the essentially meaningful part of Rosa Luxemburg's life. She was revolutionary—not in the discredited sense associated with that term today—but she lived in a politically turbulent world and had a clear vision of a path of progress that she believed would lead to a better, more peaceful world. Her belief in revolution insisted on turning away from war, which had always been considered somehow inevitable among Europeans. Part of the way we chose to get along, traditionally . . . I, too, can be discouraged by that fact.

C: It required flashbacks, however.

MvT: Yes, in order to explain what kind of relationship she had with Leo we have to look back, and at a certain point, I think one wonders what kind of child Rosa must have been. I tried to place the flashbacks about where I thought they organically would fill in the picture for the audience. I also find it more intriguing to show an effect and then turn to examine the causes. It's less linear, and I think we look at our own lives that way sometimes. Rosa's major achievements were sandwiched between two revolutions, both of them unsuccessful, but they illustrate the goals, struggles, and frustrations about other avenues of her life, which are often more elusive.

C: As a Pole and a Jew, she had two extreme disadvantages within the German party, don't you think?

MvT: Mmm, not so extreme, no. At that time, the Jews were very well assimilated in Germany. That's why I avoided putting a strong focus on the fact that she was Jewish. From today's point of view, it seems more powerful a factor than it was. I had a discussion about this with Rudolf Arnhelm, the German film historian and theoretician. He said to me, "At that time, we intellectual bourgeois Jews were totally assimilated. Nobody made an issue of it. We were no loner religious: we were integrated and secularized. We had Christmas trees . . ."

C: Yes, that scene around the Christmas tree raises more than a few eyebrows.

MvT: That's why I included it. At the beginning of the century, German Jews were quite different from the Jews in other countries, particularly here in the US where they had immigrated. In part, in order to preserve their traditions. A certain level of German Jews participated in a political climate where religion had the least impact. Particularly if they were communists or leftists. But even the run of the mill bourgeoisie took little notice of Jews as a special case, and Jews had no foresight of how it would be used against them.

C: How did she fit in then as a Pole?

MvT: She had a light accent, which Barbara Sukowa recapitulates, but her German was excellent. When I read her works today, it strikes me that she wrote a more modern German than her peers, because it is less laden with literary affectations and clunky phrasing. Clara Zetkin and Kautsky are today impossible to read without an understanding of the nineteenth-century underpinnings of purple flourishes and dry density. Rosa Luzemburg is clear, precise, and strikingly appropriate to modern politics.

It's also significant that the idea of internationalism held sway in socialist circles so she was all the more welcome. Whatever private comment was made cannot be determined and I refuse to speculate on the gossip about "that Polish Jewess" or "Red Rosa." We must remember that Bebel was defending her when he said, "red Rosa is not as terrible as they say. I couldn't do without this troublemaker in my party."

C: Didn't internationalism take a turn for the worse in Rosa's time?

MvT: She believed very strongly in it as did others, which brought them a terrible disappointment in 1914. It was the death knell of internationalism and the defeat of the Social Democratic Party in Europe. Its generosity was laid waste by the chauvinistic patriotism of war. It was the lowest point in Rosa's life. Their utopia was lost.

C: You portray that event as a rather brief indulgence in suicidal impulses.

MvT: Well, it was the realization that her function was no longer valid. I portrayed her appearance at the international Congress, where she is physically incapable of rising to address the madness she sees before her, like a Cassandra. She saw in that moment that they would all march to war together, no matter how senseless it was. That's why her speech fails her.

C: Did her sudden incapacity cause her colleagues to distrust her? Did they find her weakness feminine?

MvT: Leo accused her of that, until she explains to him. I didn't find it elsewhere, but I also believe nobody had time for that kind of pettiness. Events were moving too quickly to permit that kind of cabal. There is a line she wrote from that period that compelled me to believe in her and to make this film. In 1914 the Party had voted for war credits, and Clara and Rosa hopelessly were reduced to suicide—seriously. But Rosa advanced to the next logical thought in such an instance, "If we commit suicide, who will carry on?" So they carried on, even though the task was greater than they could imagine.

C: What role does Rosa Luxemburg play in modern Germany?

MvT: You know the story about the West German government issuing a Rosa Luxemburg commemorative stamp which nobody wanted to buy and expressly rejected. The film, on the other hand, was better received. I believe for two reasons: first, I concentrated on her struggle against war and militarism, and those scenes found a resonance among German viewers: secondly, her struggle within her own party, the Social Democrats, which is also rather relevant to modern German politics.

C: How would you compare Rosa Luxemburg's politics to those of the Federal Republic of Germany?

MvT: She always accused her political opponents of never having a clear program. And what do we have today? Parties that accept compromise after compromise until they find themselves in an arms battle in the middle of something they don't believe in. Then, they backtrack but they think they can contain the problems. Young people immediately recognized the parallel, and when she speaks of freedom or peace, young German audiences are appreciative, because they hear that nowhere else, or, at least, not in public debate. The tragedy is that the dialog that should have taken place before the First World War is still trying to take place.

C: Were you personally attacked for the film's political views?

MvT: The German press attacked me to a certain degree. Reviews were quite mixed, with some arguing that I was too sentimental and emotional in the context of a political narrative. They also claimed that this and that was missing, that I was short on history, too long on biography. But what struck me was that the academics and historians were loath to attack my "history" than were the critics, who became instant "Rosa Luxemburg Experts." They were adolescent attempts to show me what I had omitted, as if I had created this film by totally neglecting my research. It was appalling how little understanding or respect many critics had of film as a medium for opening up history rather than turning into a didactic medium. It is the Luxemburg specialists who have defended me, pointing out that as an artist, I have the right to interpret her life to choose what I show. But that's not unusual in Germany.

C: Did anyone ever say that the film depicts the dilemma of modern West Germany, with Luxemburg as an example of a voice in our wilderness?

MvT: If that were the case, nobody would ever express it in such a clear way. For example, when I was looking for funding for *Marianne and Juliane*, I went to every television station, but did ever a single one reject my proposal because it was political? Never! Nobody dared say, "The story involved a taboo theme, and you may not make it." Instead, they talked about dramaturgy and plausibility of sisters such as these and blah, blah, blah. Nobody would say simply, "I find this a politically dangerous film." That's what I mean by the way criticism is deflected into whining petulance. I probably know better than anyone what is missing or doesn't work in my own films. And that's why I wanted to practice my art so long before assaulting Rosa Luxemburg. Perhaps it was premature for my talents. But it was not premature for today's politics. It had to be done.

Red Eyes in the Cinema: Interview with Filmmaker Margarethe von Trotta about Her Anti-mafia Film, *Zeit des Zorns*

Der Spiegel / 1994

From *Der Spiegel* 4/1994, January 24, 1994. Interview conducted in German.
Translated by Monika Raesch. Reprinted by permission of *Der Spiegel*.

Spiegel: Ms. von Trotta, your new film, *Zeit des Zorns*, gives the impression that Italy's politics, economics, and military are controlled by criminals. How did the Italians react to a German filmmaker telling a narrative of a corrupt [Italian] state?[1]
Margarethe von Trotta: I could never have made this film by myself. It would have been pure arrogance on my part to judge the situation. But the screenplay was written by an Italian—

S:—the journalist Felice Laudadio.
vT: And all I added was my directing expertise.

S: Italian audiences accepted that?
vT: Nobody attacked me openly, but I had the feeling that I went too far.

S: Do you think that's the reason for the film not being successful in Italy?
vT: I guess a different reason. The film includes a few politically sensitive moments, such as the innuendo about former President Andreotti with the mafia. All officials connected with the cinema [industry] were Andreotti supporters.

S: Do you believe that *Zeit des Zorns* became a victim of a mafia-boycott?
vT: All that is needed is to "suggest" to cinema owners and distributors that the film should not be screened. Such a "suggestion" is not a direct threat, but Italians understand it.

S: Do you have any proof?

vT: No, only strong indications. At the film's premiere in Palermo, there was so much tension in the room that people stood up spontaneously and shared their personal stories. We had invited a thousand guests, among them many widows of mafia victims as well as attorneys and their bodyguards. One woman stated that her husband was murdered. He was a simple official who did not want to be(come) corrupt. She turned to the audience and yelled: "You all know the murderers."

I had the feeling: if this continues in this manner, the film will have an impact.

S: But it didn't continue in this way.

vT: Many cinemas had already booked the film. Following the premiere, they cancelled their bookings; first cinemas in Sicily, then others as well, all big first-run cinemas.

S: Perhaps the movie isn't as strong as you believe it to be.

vT: Audience reactions suggest otherwise. We spoke with audience members following the premiere. Also that other cinemas wanted to screen the film, but distributors refused to provide them with a copy.

S: Your film's main character is the doctor, Carla. Watching TV, she finds out that her husband became the victim of an assassination. But you omit her immediate reaction to this news.

vT: There are moments for which even the greatest filmmaker cannot find visuals. I prefer to give those moments to the imagination of the audience. I even believe that the audience experiences stronger feelings when the filmmaker omits details.

S: At other times, you are very particular though. *Zeit des Zorns* is dominated by close ups.

vT: I wanted to emphasize the aftermath of violence on the inner lives of my characters. Media only report about the spectacular moments of an assassination. But what about the fear of the women who know that their husband was the target of a mafia assassin? How will they live with that constant tension?

S: By now, the New German Cinema is a quarter-century old. Why didn't more come out of [this movement], something that stabilizes [the industry] for the long term?

vT: Every art has its fruitful periods followed by those where nothing appears to happen. The history that Germany currently lives was shocking to many, and it will take time to get some distance before art can be created as a reaction [to historical happenings].

S: Didn't the auteur concept—one person can and does it all, script, directing, editing—inhibit the development of film education that would train newcomers on a larger scale?

vT: Germany adopted the auteur concept from the French, from the Nouvelle Vague, simply because there was no other option. Who would have paid for a screenwriter? The desperate need for material pushed us to produce it all ourselves. Consequently, a particular style emerged, and suddenly the auteur film was the big deal.

Of course, at some point, one should have thought to build an infrastructure for those who come next. That never happened [in Germany].

S: There are more men than women among the younger filmmakers who succeeded nonetheless. Why is that?

vT: Most men don't go and watch a movie if they know ahead of time that it was directed by a female. By now, I have accepted this, even though I find that men have reason enough to be interested in a woman's viewpoint. But they don't agree.

S: It can't be that bad. Dorris Dörrie, for instance, has to attribute some of her success to male audience members.

vT: I know that I will never reach certain men with the movies I make, because they can't relate to the feelings I describe—they don't know them or don't want to know them. Other men would never admit that they cried during a screening of my movies, even as their eyes are puffy red when the lights turn back on in the theater.

S: Young female directors, such as Katja von Gernier, make it a point to explicitly distance themselves from female-made movies of the seventies and early eighties. The films are humorless, too sentimental, too serious.[2]

vT: Many people who approach me say that my movies changed their lives. That's important to me. A taxi driver even threw me out of his cab when he realized that I was the director of *Sheer Madness*. He screamed: "Out! My wife wanted to leave me after watching the movie."

At some point, one has to accept oneself and what one can do. I would love to shoot a comedy. Nonetheless, whenever it is time to decide on the next project, I select a more serious piece.

S: And the chasm between you and the younger [audiences]?

vT: I can't make movies for children who have experienced a completely different socializing process from my own. Young people today live with advertising, videos, comics, and surf TV channels. Their perception skills have accelerated. I can't nor do I want to satisfy such an audience expectation.

S: But the young people are the largest portion of the cinema audience—and they want Hollywood products.

vT: But do they really need these kinds of films? Hollywood imposes new desires onto audiences.

S: That's different in your films?

vT: I still have the hope that my movies are about actual desires and feelings. Should there be no movies for people who want to watch movies like mine? Should we not tell our stories anymore at all? If the American cinema truly conquers the entire world market, nobody will report about life in China, in Africa anymore—or even from our own lives. That's colonialism.

S: Your next movie is about a German-German love story, following the characters from the sixties until the fall of the [Berlin] Wall. Is this sort of a sequel to Christa Wolf's early novel *Der geteilte Himmel*?[3]

vT: If the title hadn't already been taken, I would have loved to use the title for my movie. Peter Schneider, who wrote the screenplay, and I included one idea present in the novel: in Christa Wolf's story, the young woman decides to remain in East Germany, because it is the harder path to follow. We now ask the question whether choosing the harder road is valuable in itself.

S: You mean scolding socialism?

vT: Being in my late sixties, it certainly isn't the movie we would have shot just a few years ago, but is a film that is very critical of socialism.

S: Today, that's a cheap criticism.

vT: Some time ago, people did not want to believe many things, even just because it was published by the Springer Press.[4] Many things we also couldn't know. Perhaps we were scared to ask the right questions—and partially so that we protected those with whom we were friends in the DDR.[5] We have to admit this failure.

Notes

1. *Zeit des Zorns* is also known as *Il lungo silenzio* and has not received an official English title.

2. The journalist uses the word "schwerblütig," which besides meaning "serious" adds the additional connotation of "ponder one's thoughts and actions for a long period of time, appearing to be performing slowly."

3. Christa Wolf's book was first published in 1963 and is available in English under the title *They Divided the Sky: A Novel by Christa Wolf.* It focuses on a relationship that is tested by the gradual development of the Berlin Wall, which was erected in 1961.

4. The Axel Springer Press is one of the largest publishing houses in Europe. It houses the *Bild Zeitung*—a popular newspaper, and *Die Welt*—a critically acclaimed newspaper, among many other brands and publications.

5. Deutsche Demokratische Republik (DDR), also referred to as East Germany before the German reunification.

Untitled Interview with Volker Schlöndorff and Margarethe von Trotta

Argos Films / 2001

From Argos Films and ARTE Développement, 2001. Producer: Florence Dauman. Transcribed by Josephine Anes; edited and formatted by Monika Raesch. The transcription includes summary statements of video excerpts and time markers. Printed by permission of Argos Films.

Margarethe von Trotta: I met Volker Schlöndorff in '69. It was then or a few months later, that he talked to me about this novel, which I wasn't familiar with, because Marguerite Yourcenar was not very well-known in Germany at the time. But having been in France, he had read her before, and he gave me the book to read. But in '69, we had just gone through '68. We were focused on other things. More on current events, on our own times, and the story seemed a little remote to me. Besides, I come from a Baltic family, I'm from noble blood, and my family comes from there. We even have a chateau, an old fortress in that region. I heard about it my whole childhood, so I was a little fed up with it. So I wasn't interested at that time.

Volker Schlöndorff: *Coup de Grâce* by Marguerite Yourcenar is one of the many novels I read when I was twenty-two or twenty-three, when I was an assistant in Paris. I remember that at the time it struck me more than others, though they were also beautiful. I had no experience with what Yourcenar called passion, romantic or otherwise. But it was this very difficult relationship in the book, or which promised to be difficult, between men and women, that struck me. Perhaps basically the impossibility of living together.

M: Volker and I collaborated in many different ways. I started with him in *Baal*, Brecht's first play in '69, in which I was only an actress. The second film was *The Sudden Wealth of the Poor People of Kombach*. I collaborated on that, or rather I assisted with the script. I wasn't really writing with him yet, but I did the historical and literary research. I would bring him the material and he would work on it. I acted in the next film. I wrote the script with him and played the leading role. Then I was assistant director. So there was a wide range of collaboration. And on *The Lost Honor of Katharina Blum*, it was the script and directing.

V: We lived together for twenty years, and we were married for seventeen of those, I think. So we were midway into our life and work together. And it reminded me a lot of *Coup de Grâce*, as if I had read it as a premonition the first time. It was our relationship.

M: In '74 the idea resurfaced. I reread the book, and I thought again about this character of Sophie. She's disturbing, fascinating, and very interesting. That's when I said "Yes, now I'd like to play her."

V: Margarethe was the soul, the very origin of the film, so I didn't need to look for my leading character. For me she was Sophie . . . because she had this unshakeable, implacable side, and we were, she more than I, extremely politically conscious—autumn of '75 in Germany, you know—and at the same time she had this exuberance.

M: I could see it was a role I wanted to do because I had wanted to be a director since the very beginning when I studied in Paris, and after seeing the films of Ingmar Bergman. I had the desire but didn't know how to make it happen. I knew that this might bring me closer to the moment when I could. I wanted to play Sophie also because I felt it would be my last role as an actress, and I wanted it to be a strong one, a character who is radical yet sensitive and vulnerable.

V: Margarethe needed a role like this. For better or worse, I had to expose our life to this challenge.

B&W photograph (@ 5:25–5:32) of Margarethe and Volker

M: When you live together, you're always talking about what you're doing. So our emotional relationship surely helped us. When my son was little, he said, "All they ever do is talk about film." So we didn't just have our working hours together, as you might have with a screenwriter or when you work with a stranger. We talk when we eat, when we go for walks. It's an ongoing process. I also think we're more free to criticize one another. You know the other person loves you and that you can be much more direct in your criticism. There's no need to be so careful about offending or upsetting someone. On the other hand, there's also the temptation to be cruel. Sometimes you mix the emotional and the professional too much. And from the moment you become involved together emotionally, you put that in the work process, too. And you have to be careful about that. In this film, it was good because it was going in the right direction. (laughs)

V: One day, at the festival in Benalmadena, where I was presenting *Fire in the Straw* with Margarethe von Trotta, I ran into producer Anatole Dauman—*B&W photograph of two men (Volker and Dauman), one with a cigarette pointing, the other with glasses (@ 7:16–7:22)*—whom I knew through friends in Paris, the same old group. He was the producer on *Hiroshima* and *Night and Fog*, and also the co-producer on *Last Year at Marienbad*, on which I had been an assistant. Anatole, who was incredibly intuitive, when it came to relationships, felt that Margarethe and I had a very creative and extremely fertile tension between us. He said, "You should do another film with her right away."

M: We wrote the first version with Jutta. But for Anatole Dauman, who was more inclined toward Erich Lhomond, as was Yourcenar, he wanted Geneviève Dormann, who was more—She was a writer and a novelist, not just a screenwriter. I think he was right to ask for her, because she prevented us from modernizing it too much. So she reworked the script. Then Volker also reviewed it with me. So it's a blend of all our temperaments.

V: I didn't participate in the writing. Margarethe worked with Geneviève Dormann, who was the perfect writer to adapt Yourcenar's novel, since Geneviève also deals with strong women in her own books, and Margarethe's focus is on strong women as well. Then there were little things I would find here and there in literature, as always. Namely Salomon and his book *Le Questionnaire*. The episode with the prisoner of war who is to be executed because he's a Bolshevik is an episode taken from Salomon and added to Yourcenar.

@ 9:41 Woman walks through a door with a scarf over her head and places it on her shoulders and walks to the other room where a man is sitting at a desk. The man gets up and enters the other room and puts his jacket on, cuts to the woman looking in the mirror. The two exchange dialogue (no subtitles), the man leaves as three others enter from another room. Cut back to Volker @ 10:47.

V: (*speaking over the scene*) Because there's one thing in Yourcenar. She always talks about the civil war in the background and the horrors of war, but it's never very concrete. In a film, when you show historic events on-screen, we want to know who the enemy is, who the adversaries are, and how the battle is fought. Everything becomes so concrete. Film demands specificity, so Margarethe and I added—partially out of political conviction as well—the whole part about the struggle of the Bolsheviks against the white officers in that era. That was not really addressed in the novel.

(cut back to Volker)

I find that once casting is done and you have all the actors, the actor becomes more important than the role. You have to adapt the role to the actor, and not vice versa, once casting is done. Because every film is a documentary, or at least a document about that actor. What the camera sees is not the acting. That's the performance. That's what's constructed. But the camera also sees the man or the woman.

@ 11:25 Cut to scene with woman sitting down with a cigarette.

Woman: Responsibility and discipline! Everything else inside you is dead. You're incapable of passion! *(cutting back and forth between Erich and woman as the man walks to the door, then pausing as the woman speaks)* You cling so tightly to life, Erich.

Erich re-enters the room and walks towards the woman, touching her on the shoulder. The two walk outside, and look up at an airplane, which crashes down into a building, and the woman, after going back inside, runs to the man, who holds her, and the two fall to the ground and begin to kiss. Erich then leaves. Scene ends @ 13:05.

V: *(begins to speak over the scene @ 12:00)* Matthias Habich, who plays the officer, Erich von Lhomond, is an actor I had not seen in the theater, though he is first and foremost a stage actor. I saw him in a political thriller for German TV, in which he was excellent. When I met him, I was struck by his French culture. He was perfectly bilingual, like myself. He had a French finesse and sensitivity, and at the same time the so-called German directness. So we felt he and Margarethe would make the perfect couple.

(cut back to Margarethe)

M: You never really know if he's looking for Sophie in the image of the brother or if he's looking for the brother in Sophie. It's very ambiguous.

V: Mathieu Carrière was a must for this film. Because of *Young Törless*, *The House of the Bories* and others, he was still—and still is—perfect to play a German officer. But also because of the places where we had filmed *Törless* and of the friendship between us.

@ 13:51 Cut to a scene with two men and the woman (who is sitting as the two men are standing, looking at one another). One man is holding out a box of cigarettes, the other man takes one and the two men begin to smoke. End scene @ 14:30.

(cut back to Volker)
V: *(speaking over the scene)* Sometimes you want to work with an actor but there is no role for him. He couldn't play Erich opposite Margarethe. It was a question of age. He couldn't be the brother either. So I had him play the angel of death who makes a brief appearance, an apparition in the film, and disappears again into death. A romantic role that suits him well.
(scene ends, cut back to Volker)

I had known Marc Eyraud for a very long time, back from my days as an assistant not only in film but also in the theater. I worked in Paris at the Théâtre Moderne with Sasha Pitoëff and his company, and Marc Eyraud was one of the pillars of that company, be it in *Uncle Vanya* or *The Seagull*. He was the perfect Chekhovian doctor, with his sadness, his melancholy and his irony too.

@ 15:03 A man is sitting down with a winter jacket and hat, drinking a shot of something. Cut to the interior of a building with bunk-beds (perhaps some sort of medical tent/hospital), with several men in it, and an officer and a man in a white coat (same as the one taking the shot from previous cut) walk out of the room into a kitchen

V: *(talking over the scene, stopping when the two men begin to speak)* I find that he too strays a bit from the character as written by Yourcenar. But he creates a perfectly credible character in its place.

Man in white: It's impossible to go on like this
Officer: What's the situation?
Man in white: No more alcohol or morphine. For weeks without typhus vaccine. I've opened the last box of dressing. *(man is pouring liquid into a glass and handing it to the officer)*
Officer: I know. We couldn't bring any. Konrad cabled Riga yesterday.
Man in white: Meanwhile, I'm in this mess.
Scene ends @ 15:39, just as the officer takes his drink

(cut back to Volker)
V: We took small liberties in casting, which of course, always changes the nature of a book. It can't be otherwise. You can't construct an actor ready-made to fit perfectly a great role in literature. You always have to go by the flesh-and-blood actors and actresses you have and see how you can adapt the book to them.

@ 16:10 A man escorts a woman (Aunt Praskovia) in black to a seat, surrounded by a crowd of men clapping and she sits down.

V: *(talking over the scene)* There's an amazing character in the film: Aunt Praskovia, who goes way beyond what's in the novel. She's played by Valeska Gert.

Aunt Praskovia begins to sing.
Aunt Praskovia: *(singing)* To have some fun, to play around—*(spoken)* You're behind—Wonderful. Then, when it ends, a whirling waltz—Faster—He held me against his heart, so tight against his heart. You gentlemen, all my cavaliers, you are my passion, and you too, young lieutenant, I love you too. He twirled his moustache, he twirled me around. *(a man and women are shown dancing)*
Scene ends @ 17:28.

(cut back to Volker)
V: It was part of her repertoire, and in yet another moment of madness I decided that she reminded me so much of silent Expressionist cinema that having the opportunity to record that was more important than remaining absolutely faithful to the novel.

@ 17:52 Cut to woman (Valeska) dancing; Margarethe speaks over clip. Clip ends at 18:06.

M: She had been a great diva of silent movies, after all. She was in *Joyless Street* and other films *(cut back to Margarethe)*. She was always very exaggerated, every expressionistic.

V: I found her at her dressing table. She was putting on eye shadow, one eye all violet-blue, the other a greenish color. I said to her, "Valeska, you do know we're filming in black and white." "I don't give a damn what you're filming in. I'm not doing it for you. I'm doing it for me. I think I look sad and pale, so I'm putting on white so I'll be even more white and pale. Then I'm adding a little color to cheer me up a bit."

M: She was really from the era in which the film is set, the twenties. We were from the era in which it was filmed. She was from the twenties, and she struck a tone in the film that was absolutely fantastic. I remember her hair, for example. She always had very greasy hair. The makeup artist didn't want to touch her anymore. She told her, "Please, wash your hair this once." Finally she did, but as soon as her makeup was on, she put hair grease back in her hair to achieve that look, that punk look. She was punk before punk was in style.

V: It was great to go back ten years later to the place where I had filmed *Törless*, which was very close to my heart. I felt like I was coming home by returning to that region. All the more since I was with Igor Luther (*cut to photograph of Luther @ 20:18*), the director of photography on the film, with whom I was finally going to work. I say finally because I had known him for over ten years (*cut to another picture @ 20:26 of a group of people around a camera*), having met him in '68 in Czechoslovakia (*cut back to Volker @ 20:34*). He was a young cameraman working with Jakubisko. I thought he was great. Back then, he wouldn't work with me. In the meantime, he had fled the Russians and settled in Munich. I had a great friendship and fondness for Igor during all those years because we share the same passion for Soviet silent cinema, especially Dovzhenko's films. He was from Slovakia, just some sixty miles from where we were going to film. So he, too, was going home to the country of his roots and the light that he knew so well.

@ 21:20 A car is driving down a road, a man shoots his gun into the woods, gets out and runs to pick up the bird/animal he killed. The men get back into the car and drive off, having a conversation.

V: (*talking over the scene*) The cold and gray weather we had during filming, with glacial winds and temperature of fifteen or twenty [degrees Celsius] below zero, didn't scare us. This was the climate of his native land and therefore mild to him. And for me it was the landscape of Törless.

Narration: (*starts @ 21:50*) We went to Riga to discuss the details of the next offensive. We learned that the Allies favored the Soviets, depriving our obstinate resistance of all meaning.
Man 1: Careful of the ice. Imagine being killed in a car.
Man 2: During the war! (*laughs*)
The men drive up to and through a gate, passing two people, one with a bike, nearly running them over. Scene ends @ 22:28.

M: Yes, filming in the cold was sometimes very difficult. We were far from everything, in Austria, near the Hungarian border. We had found this marvelous château. It was a little like a Baltic château. It was sometimes so cold and my face was so stiff that I was afraid I wouldn't find the right facial expression. I have it inside me, but I felt my face wasn't going along.

V: The film is in black and white, naturally, since it's a war film, and a period piece. So black and white was a must. But there are other reasons: First, I love black and white. From time to time in between films, I've gone back to black-and-white photography. In this case, in *Coup de Grâce*, I think it was essential to use black and white because of the faces. In color, the eyes don't stand out. You focus on a spot of red or some other color somewhere else. Black and white—and we know this from Bergman's film—looks into the soul. It looks at the eyes, and through the eyes, into the character. It was so important here because, as Heinrich Böll said, "The film is the story of one woman's face, Sophie's face, surrounded and framed by men's faces," be it those of the officers or the revolutionaries. All men's faces. And black and white helps with that. Igor Luther is a director of photography who also comes from black and white. From a Russian or Soviet school or background, if you will. We did tests, even using sound stock—14 ASA, used for optical sound—which we used for some night scenes and battle scenes, mostly at the end. (*fade to black*)

The film was edited by Henri Colpi, the great editor who is also the director of *The Long Absence*. He had worked many times with my producer, Anatole Dauman, who asked him to return to editing and make this film with me. It was absolutely marvelous, and, as often happens, when we finished filming, I hated everything we had shot. I thought it was worthless. It didn't express anything. There's often the risk of going into the cutting room and destroying everything you filmed because you're too close to it. You can't see its qualities. Henri Colpi literally banished me from the cutting room. I had begun an edit with a German editor in which I was literally destroying the film with very short cuts and all that. He banned me from the cutting room. He viewed the rushes again and started over from scratch. He gave the film the rhythm it had while we were filming. He didn't work against the current. He really worked with the grain of the film, with remarkable sensitivity. It was very much in line with Stanley Myers, the musician, with whom I'd made many films and who died a few years ago. His music for this film had a Bartok-like feeling to it. Because the landscape where we filmed, which was the same as where we filmed *Young Törless*, for me it was the music of Bartok. Stanley always feels the music should be very minimal. Wherever you can do without, there should be none. No long streams that go on and on. Just accents, moments. And especially, of course, not at the end. You can't set music to an execution. Otherwise it becomes opera, which is a different art form. But not in film. So it was one of Stanley Myers's most beautiful compositions. What wasn't in the credits, because we didn't know it at the time, was that Hans Zimmer was Stanley Myers's assistant and therefore worked behind the scenes on the music for *Coup de Grâce*.

@ 27:41 Scenes with officers running with a horse
Dedication appearing on screen:

To my first master,	Meinem ersten Lehrer
Jean-Pierre Melville	Jean Pierre Melville gewidmet
V.S.	V.S.

End scene @ 27:48

(*cut back to Volker*)
V: The dedication to Jean-Pierre Melville says it also. I was writing to my first teacher, although Alain Resnais and Louis Malle mostly were my teachers. Louis was more than a teacher, he was a brother. But I learned a lot from Melville. I learned to be extremely thrifty when making films.

@ 28:14 Cut to a picture of two men, one in an officer's uniform, with the caption: Jean-Pierre Melville Volker Schöndorff

(*cut back to Volker @ 28:26*)
V: He made his movies with next to nothing. In black and white, in his own studio. If a table and chair were needed on a set, there was a table and chair and nothing else. He was always seeking the minimum without making it into an aesthetic statement. *The Godson* is a prime example of this. But the minimum in terms of crew as well, in terms of everything involved in a film. His minimum crew was Henri Decaë and himself. Later it was Nicolas Hayer or other cameramen. When I make films like *Young Törless*, *Coup de Grâce*, or recently *Legend of Rita*, I always apply the lesson I learned from Jean-Pierre Melville. How to do with the minimum?

@ 29:29 cut to title card that reads:
Le Coup De Grace
d'après le roman de
Marguerite Yourcenar
Editions Gallimard
Ends @ 29:27

(cut back to Volker)

V: What gives the writing in the novel such extraordinary power is that behind the novel you sense a real lived experience. Very often, when you adapt books, you find behind the book a secret energy. *(cut to a picture of the book "Le Coup du Grâce")*

Marguerite Yourcenar uses this, namely for the three main characters. Sophie, Erich von Lhomond, and Konrad formed a constellation, "a real occurrence," as she says, that somebody had told her about. But it still wasn't her own experience. But now that we know that when she wrote the book she had just met Grace in Italy, you understand that her relationship with Grace, which was to last thirty or forty years, was the "real story" that gave the book its underlying energy. *(cut to a letter from Volker to Marguerite Yourcenar)*

I corresponded with Marguerite Yourcenar, and always by mail. We never managed to meet her.

(cut to Margarethe)

M: I tried to contact Marguerite Yourcenar. I wrote her that I was coming to New York and was very interested in meeting her. But she advised strongly against it. She said it was very far, that she lived on an island off of Maine, that it was complicated to get there and it was very cold. She set so many obstacles in my path that I understood she didn't want to meet, so I didn't insist.

V: Madame Yourcenar answered, "There's no need to come see me. We're in agreement on all points. I don't see what further discussion could contribute." We were very surprised at the time, as well as a little bit worried and annoyed. What did this mean? Was she distancing herself from the project? It was only when I read her biography years later that I realized how, that very week, the friend with whom she had lived for thirty or forty years was seriously ill and on her deathbed. This friend's name was Grace, and thus *Coup de Grâce* is about Grace. It's the book she wrote when she met Grace in 1939. The double meaning in the title is very profound. When Margarethe was about to play Grace, the real Grace was on her deathbed, and Yourcenar didn't want to meet us at that moment.

M: What interested us most in the text was Sophie, unlike Marguerite Yourcenar, for whom Erich Lhomond was the character with whom she most identified, much more than Sophie. We inverted the story a little. We made Sophie the main role because she seemed more modern. As Yourcenar said in one of her texts, he is a Racinian character: noble and somewhat pitiful. Whereas Sophie is looking for something. She wants something. She's looking for love. She wants to fulfill herself as a woman, and as a fighter at the end. This seemed more relevant to our times.

V: Who's telling the story in *Coup de Grâce*? In the novel, it's very clear. Erich von Lhomond tells the story in a train station—in Pisa I think. In the film, you don't need this narrator's perspective. Because of the history of World War II, I couldn't have identified with a right-wing officer as a narrator.

M: Those men who fought at the time against the Russian and the Reds became Nazis when they returned to Germany. We mustn't forget that. It may not have been Erich Lhomond, Youcenar's character, but his race and that type of officer who went there became—Whether you're writing, or reading the novel, it played a role.

V: There's one objective fact: She wrote this novel in 1939. That is, before the war. Before fascism, basically. She knew the good-natured Italian fascism whose only accomplishment was to make the trains run on time, as she says. But we made the film in '75. That is, after World War II, after the Holocaust, after all that we know about the results of fascism.

M: When you write a script, even when you write based on a novel that was written at a much earlier time, you're influenced by the era in which you live, by your private, social, and political life. All this plays a part and goes into the script and into the film. If we were to make this film today, it might be completely different. Not in terms of the story line—you can't change the story of a novel. But in terms of interpretation, I think we would change some things.

@ 36:22 Cut to a train moving down its track towards the frame/camera. It passes by and the camera shifts to two officers with guns and people being escorted away from the tracks. The person kneels and the officer shoots the person. Several gun shots are heard. A woman, after talking with an older man, walks over to where the bodies are; the man runs to other officers by the train
Man: She demands—The young lady requests—She'd like you to do it.
The man walks over to the woman, she moves behind a shed, and is executed.
Officer: (*after killing the woman*) Line up for a picture.
The officers line up for a picture and get back on the train, pulling away.
Cuts to text @ 39:41.

V: (*talking over scene*) The train arriving at the end of the film was a Hungarian train that they rented to us from behind the Iron Curtain, and that we used as is, with the locomotive at the back, because that's how it arrived. From the moment the train arrives at the station to the time it leaves again had to be a single shot to show the executions as very mundane, just another task to take care of before catching the train. Not a big production. A trivial event in a train station. Line them up against the wall. One, then the next, next, next. A bullet to the back of the head and let them drop. So the style here is that of a documentary, and at the same time it's relevant to our era. That was the solution to how not to get in too close, to not get into the psychology of the execution scene.

(*after dialogue between man and officer*) I purposely did not use a close up, because I think decency prohibits showing in close up the ultimate moment when someone dies or is executed. It would be obscene to show that with makeup and trick photography and special effects. It's an almost unspeakable thing, and therefore the camera is very far away.

(*after execution*) All aboard. Farewell group photo. Everybody smile. The train leaves. That's how it stands for the view; and for us who filmed it and for the actors who played it: In the span of two minutes, twelve people are executed. A train pulls in and pulls out again. The banality of it. The whole thing is reduced to the dimension of a trivial incident. A tragedy in the literary sense. A trivial incident in terms of the story.

@ 39:41 text appears on screen: "At first I thought that in asking me to play executioner, she wished to give me final, conclusive proof of her love. Later I understood her sole aim was revenge, to leave me prey to remorse. She was right in that: I do feel remorse at times. One is always trapped somehow in deals with women."

(*cut back to Margarethe @ 40:00*)
M: The text at the end is taken from Yourcenar's novel, but we in Germany didn't put it in. It was Anatole Dauman, the French co-producer, who wanted it in, because it was also his point of view on Erich and on the story. Maybe it was a good thing, because this way he brought the story back to the struggle between the sexes. I don't know. Today I'd say he was right. At the time he did it, I was a little—I thought you couldn't look at it that way. It was seeing it too much from the man's perspective. But I think he was right.

V: When she says, "I want Erich to be the one who executes me," that could be viewed as a final declaration of love. She knows her death is inevitable. She is to be executed just like her companions. She wants to spend this last moment of her life with him by her side. Death might prove easier in his presence. The fact that he holds the revolver makes it somehow easier for her to die. That's the generous view. It can also be read as defiance. "If I must die, I want him to be the one to kill me because I know it will leave an indelible mark on him. He will never get over it." It's not to make him feel guilty, but literally, "If I force him to kill me, he will be the one destroyed."

M: I don't agree on that point either. It's not revenge on her part. It's her request that he fire the gun rather than let some other solider do it. She wants to make an imprint on his memory.

V: So is it the second interpretation or the first? Fortunately all we do is show it. In a film, we don't need to decide. We can leave it completely ambiguous.

Cut to black. Picture of five people at the end.

An Interview with Margarethe von Trotta, Director of *Rosenstrasse*

Richard Phillips / 2005

From *World Socialist Web Site*, http://www.wsws.org/en/articles/2005/05/rosen-m31.html, May 31, 2005. Reprinted by permission of *World Socialist Web Site*.

More than two years after its European premiere, Margarethe von Trotta's *Rosenstrasse* is finally being shown in Australian cinemas. The movie is about the courageous action of German women who protested against the arrest and impending deportation of their Jewish husbands by the Nazis in 1943. It will screen at Palace cinemas in Sydney and Melbourne in early June, with other cities to follow.

Previously reviewed by the World Socialist Web Site (*Some of Hitler's unwilling victims*), von Trotta's film is a powerful depiction of these previously little-known protests.

Defying constant fascist intimidation, the growing number of demonstrators maintained their protest day and night in late February and early March, 1943. The demonstrators' intransigence finally forced the authorities to free up to two thousand Jews, including some who had already been deported to Auschwitz. As one of *Rosenstrasse*'s central characters remarks towards the end of the film, it was "a ray of hope in a sea of darkness." Some historians estimate that up to six thousand people were involved in the demonstrations.

Von Trotta, who worked with directors Rainer Werner Fassbinder and Volker Schlöndorff during the late 1960s and '70s, has written and directed a number of award-winning films, including *The Lost Honor of Katharina Blum* (1975), *Rosa Luxemburg* (1986), *The Promise* (1995), as well as numerous television dramas. She recently spoke by phone with Richard Phillips about *Rosenstrasse*.

Richard Phillips: Firstly, let me congratulate you on an impressive and very humane film. How and why you were attracted to the subject?

Margarethe von Trotta: And so late, after all it happened in 1943. Of course, I, like most Germans, including many Berliners, had never heard of the Rosenstrasse protests and I didn't find out about them until the early 1990s, after the Berlin Wall came down.

At that time Volker Schlöndorff, who was in charge of Studio Babelsberg, heard about the story and thought it would be a good project for me because of my reputation as a so-called feminist director. He put me in touch with a documentary filmmaker—Daniela Schmidt—who'd made a movie about the demonstrations, and through her I met some of the people she'd interviewed. I was able to speak to even more people—about twelve or fifteen altogether—because some didn't want to be interviewed on camera for her film.

It was a varied group: there were some women and men, and younger people who had protested in the street with their mothers, as well as some Jewish people who had been locked up by the Nazis. I collected a whole spectrum of testimonies and spent many days with individual participants, which was very moving. As I began to more deeply understand the tremendous courage of these people, I just had to make this film.

I wrote my first script, which centered entirely on events in 1943, but Schlöndorff said it would be too expensive and that the studios couldn't afford it and that I should prune it back. So I cut it and came up with the idea of little Ruth leading us through the story. But despite this we were still unable to get the German film finance institutions to provide any money and had to give up the project. At that time, all they were interested in was comedies. We had several years of these sorts of films, which were not very sophisticated, and could not be released anywhere else in the world. Everyone thought German cinema was dead.

The 1990s was a difficult period and I wasn't able to do anything much until I got some television work, which really saved me and gave me a living.

Then, in 2001, a friend suggested that I should try to make *Rosenstrasse* again. Political times had changed, the days of German comedies were over, and we thought it might be possible to try again. So I wrote another script. I couldn't present the old one to the funding institutions; they had already rejected the initial proposal.

This time I asked Pam Katz, a New York Jewish scriptwriter, if she would like to work with me on the story, but this time starting in contemporary New York and moving back to Europe and the Nazi years. I chose New York because many Jewish people escaping the Nazis had gone to America.

The script was finally accepted and so it took more or less eight years from my initial interest until I was able to actually start shooting the film.

RP: Of the people you interviewed, who had the biggest impact and why?

MvT: While the events are true, the characters are a mixture of the people I met during the first research and my own fantasy. Lena, however, is mainly based on one person I interviewed at length. Unfortunately, she was very old and by the time I'd begun filming she was already dead. In fact, half of the people I'd met at the beginning were dead when the film finally came out, which was very sad.

RP: It seems to me that the film is an important antidote to those like Daniel Goldhagen who claim that the German people were Hitler's willing executioners.
MvT: That everyone was a hangman?

RP: Yes. Your film reveals some of the opposition that existed. Did this attract you to the subject as well?
MvT: Well, my intention was not to make a picture that answered Daniel Goldhagen. Nor was my aim to rehabilitate Germans, which would have been shameless on my part.

Of course, I don't agree with his claims that the German people willingly accepted Hitler. But the problem was that there were too few people in Germany who reacted like my women in *Rosenstrasse* or others who bravely resisted the Nazis.

For me, the main issue was to show the courage of these women, which was so amazing, and to explore the contradiction between the Nazis' firm belief in the faithfulness of women to their husbands, and the fact that that these women were being faithful to their Jewish husbands.

RP: What has been the response to the film in Germany?
MvT: The public reaction was very good. It has been my most successful film, which was very surprising, even to me. And there has been a good response wherever it has been screened—in the US, France, Italy, and Israel.

RP: Many of your films explore historical issues of the twentieth century. Why do you think this is important?
MvT: I must say that not all of my films deal with historical questions but certainly the best-known ones do. I have a reputation of being a political, historical, and feministic filmmaker, but half of my pictures have been psychoanalytical examinations of personal relationships.

But I think as a German, and from the generation that came into being towards the end of the Nazi regime, it was very important for me to explore these historical questions. I was also influenced by, and participated in, the so-called student rebellion, where the issues of the Holocaust and more details about the Nazis' record started to become known. Young people began to ask their parents what really went on in these years and whether or why they didn't rebel against Hitler's regime.

I'm particularly interested in showing aspects of these events through personal stories and exploring how and why people could accept rules and regulations that, in a different time, people could not or would not normally follow. I don't know if I've explained this very well but, for instance, I made a four-part television series in which the main character was born in Germany in March 1933. Who would pick this date if you had a choice? Do you become someone who follows orders or do you become someone who refuses to think this way and rebels in their own way? These are important questions.

RP: In the background material for *Rosenstrasse* you make reference to Walter Benjamin and an article called "The Angel of History." I'm not familiar with this. Could you elaborate?

MvT: Benjamin, as you probably know, was a German Jewish philosopher from Berlin, who went into exile in France when Hitler's regime came to power. He committed suicide in 1940 while attempting to escape to America from France. His essay is about how you always look back at history and that, although you may want to escape the past, you cannot. This has been an important inspiration and guide to me.

RP: Why do you think the film industry has taken so little interest in seriously exploring important historical issues?

MvT: It's a complex question and it doesn't just apply to history. Today, for example, you can see many, many violent films but there is no analysis of where this violence comes from.

In relationship to Germany, after the war many people didn't want to be confronted with the past. Some felt guilty, others were traumatized, and so there was a collective silence. That silence was broken in the 1960s with the student radicalization. Then there was the theory that everyone was responsible for the Nazi regime, that everyone was guilty. But, of course, when everyone is guilty no one is responsible, so this clouded the issue. It was only later in the 1990s that some examination of these questions began.

At the same time, in East Germany [where the Rosenstrasse protests actually took place], they were not really reported on and the people involved were not regarded as heroines. I suspect that in official circles they were defined as nonpolitical, that they just began these protests out of devotion to their husbands and nothing else. While the Rosenstrasse women might have started out apolitical, as more and more became involved it obviously became a political movement. Maybe if there had been communists involved, or something like that, then perhaps the East German government might have paid more attention. So these courageous individuals were largely ignored.

As you know, there are always people who want to understand and remember and those who want to repress all memories. In *Rosenstrasse* you have both tendencies. Sometimes it's difficult to confront these questions, and for some it's better to try and live in a dream world or to flee.

RP: It's impossible to watch this movie and not think about the war in Iraq and the illegal detention of hundreds of people in Guantanamo Bay and other places as part of the so-called war on terror. Could you comment on this?

MvT: I was born in Germany before the war ended and saw its terrible effects, with whole areas devastated and tremendous poverty, so I'm totally antiwar and was opposed to the invasion of Iraq. Sixty years ago, many German people regarded the American military as liberators. Few people see it that way anymore. Many think of them as the opposite. But when I began filming *Rosenstrasse* the war had not started and I didn't intend to make any comparison between these events. It's true though, there is a correspondence. Today there are many war crimes being committed, efforts to cover them up, and, no doubt, attempts to forget these crimes.

KinoSommer and Conversation with Filmmaker

chk / 2007

From *RheingauCenter Nachrichten*, May 2007. Translated by Monika Raesch.
Reprinted with permission by the publisher.

KinoSommer ["CinemaSummer"] Hessen played in Schlangenbad on Saturday.[1] While the event had to be moved from the outdoor venue Kurpark-Kollonaden to the Kursaal due to cold and unpredictable weather, the atmosphere was not impacted. Tonight's schedule was *I Am the Other Woman* (2006) by Margarethe von Trotta. A large audience, including many locals, convened to watch the movie and hear the filmmaker speak live prior to the screening. Both she and Mayor Michael Schlepper, who enjoyed dinner together prior to the event, smiled from ear to ear. "I like your mayor," she explained to the audience. "He speaks a lovely hessisch [local dialect]." Schlepper implied the filmmaker's special relationship to the city of Schlangenbad, but wanted to leave it up to her to speak about it.

That eventually happened in the live interview with media professor Dr. Astrid Pohl from nearby Marburg. "I often visited Schlangenbad with Volker Schlöndorff. We visited his father, and we got married here. Still, I vividly remember the registrar who explained that this isn't a job but a calling that leads one to the role [of becoming a registrar]. That's the same with acting. I liked that he spoke of 'calling.' Sadly, [my marriage] only lasted for twenty years." The marriage between Margarethe von Trotta and Volker Schlöndorff, who grew up in Schlangenbad, ended in divorce in 1991.

Astrid Pohl's aim was to explore the meaning the Rhine river has for the filmmaker, as it is a reoccurring feature in her films and her life. "When I was a little child—unconscious to me at the time—I only experienced the history of this country via its destructive past; I lived with my mom among the ruins of Berlin," Trotta shares. "We moved from Berlin to Bad Godesberg[2] in 1948, in a functioning world,[3] complete with Siebengebirge [a mountain range along the Rhine].

Whenever I feel bad, all I have to do is sit at the edge of the river to feel better. The saying goes, 'Father Rhine.' The Rhine is a father for me; I who grew up without a father."

"Where is your home?" Astrid Pohl asked. "I don't have a home, and if, then it is my mother who I loved very much; but no place is home. I was without any nationality until I got married. Being without a nationality also means being without a home." Today, Margarethe von Trotta lives in Paris, but doesn't live there more than approximately two months out of the year, as she is busy traveling. She visited Paris for the first time when she was eighteen; back then to study. "But I sat more in the cinema than at the university. I discovered Nouvelle Vague in Paris. I found everything that art means to me when exploring film." In 1960, she formulated her goal of becoming a director, something impossible to achieve by a woman during that time. "I became an actress with the hope to break into directing at a later time." It would be seventeen years before she could direct for the first time. "Today, you are Germany's most famous female director," Astrid Pohl states, but Margarethe von Trotta passionately protests and lists several successful German female directors. "I may be the oldest," she smirks.

Margarethe von Trotta was honored with the *Hessische Filmpreis* in 2004.[4] She shoots many of her films in the state. Last fall, she shot at the Ebersbach Monastery for her film *Vision* (2009), which will be coming to cinemas this upcoming fall. Her 2006 movie, *I Am the Other Woman*, had many scenes shot in the Rheingau area—among other locations she shot in the Ebersbach Monastery and high above Assmannshausen. The movie is about a young woman with many different personalities, a dictatorial father, an alcoholic mother, and a young man who falls in love with her. Katja Riemann, Armin Müller-Stahl, Karin Dor, and August Diehl play the main characters. "All excellent actors," Astrid Pohl remarks. She guides the interview very well, implying lots of preparation and sensibility. "This movie is a little different in comparison to my older works. It's not fully my style. But look closely; those types of people really do exist," says Margarethe von Trotta who rewatched the movie once more as well.

During the intermission, patrons could get food and beverages and chat with Margarethe von Trotta. In the meantime, Paul-Rainer Wicke and his son Adrian prepared the movie to ensure the one hundred audience members a powerful movie experience. One of the sponsors of the KinoSommer Hessen is Rheingau Echo.

Notes

1. Hessen is a particular state in Germany, and Schlangenbad is a city in Hessen.

2. Bad Godesberg is a municipal district of Bonn in mid-West Germany. Bonn was the capital of West Germany from 1949 until 1999.

3. Von Trotta used the idiom "heile Welt."

4. This award has been presented annually since 1990. It is awarded by the state of Hessen's Ministry for Science and Art (Hessisches Ministerium für Wissenschaft und Kunst).

Interview with Margarethe von Trotta (Director and Screenplay / *Vision*)

Aleksandra Majzlic / 2009

From *M Lifestyle—Das Münchner Lifestylemagazin*, www.m-lifestyle.de, 2009. Translated by Monika Raesch. Reprinted by permission of Aleksandra Majzlic and Margarethe von Trotta.

Born in Berlin, she is one of Germany's most successful female directors internationally. Following up after joint directing and screenwriting work with ex-husband Volker Schloendorff (*The Lost Honor of Katharina Blum*), she made her award-wining directorial debut with *The Second Awakening of Christa Klages* in 1977. Movies that received multiple awards, including *The Promise* and *Rosa Luxemburg* followed. In this interview, Margarethe von Trotta shares her motivational quote by Brecht, what guidance Volker Schlöndorff provides her with, and why a scream on the set can be rather productive at times.

Aleksandra Majzlic: Do you still speak with Volker Schlöndorff about your movie projects today?

Margarethe von Trotta: Yes, and I think of two statements: one by Goethe, so it is noble: "Wishes are premonitions of abilities," and the other one is "heavy," from Brecht: "It's better to produce shit than to produce nothing at all."[1] (*laughs*) That's my principle. So there are times when I say to [Volker]: "God, it's better you make the movie; you will make something worthwhile out of it, regardless of whether you have the best script of all time. But the way you make movies, something exciting and interesting will emerge, because you are so talented." I don't think it's ever good to just sit at home and be sad. Our DNA tells us to produce movies. Making movies is our life.

AM: Do you work even when you are on a holiday?

MvT: I often travel to Terracina, a town located in between Rome and Naples; a girlfriend of mine owns a house there right on the ocean. I go swimming in the morning, and then I go to my room and write. This was the very first summer I did not write a screenplay; it was wonderful. Well, I did a little bit of work. I have an offer to direct two movies for an Italian producer, so I had business meetings, read a screenplay, but did not write one myself.

AM: Are you a workaholic?

MvT: Well, yes, you can say that. But it's not like I can't be quiet or can't sit still and appreciate the stillness; not like that.

AM: As part of your previous production, you spent quite a bit of time in monasteries. Could you envision taking a spiritual break by spending time in a monastery?

MvT: Yes, absolutely. That's the bad thing, that we are no longer accustomed to quietness; and most people are scared to be alone, as they then have to focus on themselves. But that's when it gets exciting. I'm not that kind of workaholic who doesn't appreciate those moments. In the evening, before I go to sleep, I often focus and ask myself silent questions and I receive answers.

AM: Which questions do you ask yourself [silently]?

MvT: Nothing about love. I don't ask: "Is there a man around the corner waiting for me?" (*laughs*)

AM: Does religion play a role in your life?

MvT: I attend church when friends of mine are ill. I light candles for them und think about them as I stare into the flame. Of course, God enters in those moments in some way. I often say: "Thank you that this person still lives; please continue to care for him/her." I can't do the latter; all I can do is ask for it. Whether that makes a difference [in my friends' lives] I don't know. I know thousands of scientific books about this question. Analyses conclude that it doesn't make any difference. But for the people who we tell that we pray for them or light a candle for them, it feels good for them. And that positive thought process furthers healing power. It's like Hildegard said: "First you must heal the soul; only then the body can follow." I agree with that. It was very important for me to show Hildegard's position to the entire human being [in the film]. She also believed that the elements can turn against us. If we destroy nature, nature will destroy us. Only today do we realize what a modern thinker Hildegard was.

AM: During a fight, Richardis accuses Hildegard that she only communicates with the powerful to feed her ambition; it's the same ambition that drives her to write books, work to establish a monastery. . . . Is this a correct accusation? Or is the reason for her engagement due to her faith?

MvT: Most likely both. You can call it ambition if one is vicious. When women want to achieve something, it is often said that we are either hysterical or ambitious; nobody says that about a man. It is part of a man's being, being ambitious. Of course, Hildegard wanted to express her own thoughts, which was supported by her religious beliefs. Psalms, the Bible, those were her materials that also form the basis for her visions. She added her own poetic use of language, lived her own creativity in her visions. She used those visions to announce: "The lively light asked me to establish a monastery." She was very brave, acknowledging visions. And she was smart by using her knowledge of the masculine psyche to gain acknowledgment. That permitted her to say that God ordered her to do something, to establish a monastery. But basically, it was her wish.

AM: The nuns vowed that they would not leave the monastery anymore. That would mean that Richardis should not have left, correct?

MvT: That's true. But the brother's powerful position came into play. He was a man, a bishop, and ordered themm to do so, and that's why it worked. The power that rich families also exuded is something I am trying to show in the film as well. Whoever was not a noble, was a worker bee; the nobles had a comfortable life; they could study and were served. And that's why they said, when the new monastery was being built: "We didn't join [the church] to get our hands dirty." Many rebelled and a few left [the church].

AM: Concerning your work as a director, what is the importance of you having been an actress as well?

MvT: I simply know how exposed an actor feels. Many directors only spent time standing behind the camera. They think that they can move actors around like a piece of furniture. When I teach students in a directing program I always say to them: "You have to act at least once in your life so that you have an understanding of the position of an actor." For instance, when I realize that I wanted to have an actor portray something in a different direction, but the actor cannot do that, then I rather stay with him. I then have to support him to get the best out of his performance in his chosen direction; then it turns out well.

AM: Are you able to be that flexible and open-minded when you are under stress?

MvT: Yes, earlier on in my career I would leave the set, scream loudly, return, and everything was all good.

AM: Do you remain in control of your emotions on the set?

MvT: At first, some crew members' thoughts: "That's a weak woman; she isn't talented." They were used to working with men, and had the view that "one can do anything with her." When I felt that attitude, I screamed once properly and fully; one guy approached me and said, "I didn't expect that; you should do that more often." I replied: "You are so stupid, if you don't realize that I could do that, but that I don't want to do that. I want to create a good atmosphere, but that's not possible when one screams."

Notes

1. This is an unofficial translation of Brecht's words. In German, he said: "Besser Ihr macht Scheisse, als das Ihr gar nichts macht."

Margarethe von Trotta Speaks about God

Karolina Zebrowski / 2009

From *Film Reporter*, September 21, 2009. Translated by Monika Raesch.
Reprinted by permission of *Film Reporter*.

Hildegard von Bingen was always fascinated by the women's movement, Christians, and all those interested in the art of healing. Margarethe was not left untouched by this strong woman, who knew what she wanted out of life. After several years of studying the material, von Trotta decided to make a film about the "herb nun"[1]: *Vision—From the Life of Hildegard von Bingen*. It not only features a prominent German cast, but it also reflects on faith. The director spoke with us about her own personal relationship with faith. Surprising opinions surfaced.

Ricore: How do you feel after completing such an important piece [the film *Vision* (2009)]? Relieved? Or do you think about things that you wish you could have done differently?

Margarethe von Trotta: Well, throughout the entire production, I constantly thought that we should include this and that . . . Barbara Sukowa felt the same way. She continued to read and research. One day, she approached me with new scenes about sex, things about "towers" . . . It is sort of funny how Hildegard von Bingen imagines the sex act between a man and a woman. The suggestion to include this came to [Barbara] in the middle of shooting. That was not part of the original screenplay. We constantly had new ideas of what we wanted to add here and there. During post production, I had to cut some of it out as it was simply too much. One always has to be selective. Afterwards, one is tormented with the question whether one made the right selection. That torments me to this day.

R: The "enlightment" scene about sex is rather funny.

MvT: I found it in a biography, written by Barbara Beuys. She wrote: "How Volmar . . . ," who is played by Heino Ferch in our film, " . . . how he reacted when he read this and had to copy it." We included that in the film. Heino acts so wonderfully in this scene. (*laughs*)

R: How did Hildegard get her ideas? How was she informed about sex?
MvT: I don't know. I am sure that she read a lot when practicing homeopathic medicine or when she worked at the hospital and when she spoke with doctors. She could envision many things. We all asked ourselves that [question]. Where does a nun receive that information? To describe a penis as a small tower between two buildings that functions as a support structure (*laughs*) . . .

R: You had the idea to make this film a long time ago. What was the trigger that finally brought this project to life?
MvT: I had this idea at the beginning of the 1980s for the first time. That wasn't my crazy idea though; rather it was a result of the women's movement that already occurred at the beginning of the century. Post 1968, more women's groups formed who researched: what was the status of women in the past; what did they do? We were not taught any of this in school back then. In religion class, if at all, only the saints would maltreat themselves for their beliefs. We never were presented with strong women. We searched all the way into mythology. That's when Hildegard von Bingen surfaced for the first time. I thought, we have to create a project about this woman. I didn't have faith in the producers though to pull that off.

R: The project fell apart because of financing issues?
MvT: Well, I couldn't imagine being able to find enough money for that type of project. But that's my fault. I didn't even attempt to succeed. At some point, I told my current producer, Markus Zimmer, about that idea. That was when I had planned to make a film about Hannah Arendt. He suggested focusing on Hildegard von Bingen. Do you know who Hannah Arendt was?

R: Hmmm . . .
MvT: A super intellectual woman of the last century. Markus thought that nobody wanted to see anything about her life. I told him that if he wanted Hildegard von Bingen and would permit me to write the screenplay that I would do so gladly. I didn't want to waste my time developing something and then not having it go into production, the way it happened with Hannah Arendt. After all, I have to earn a living. I think he thought the timing was right for that movie. It is often the case that producers know that better than directors.

R: How did you internalize the religious aspects of the story?
MvT: We were all raised as Christians. It's not like I was born an atheist. My mom

believed, and I attended a Diakonie boarding school.[2] I am a Protestant and was raised with many Christian values. I studied art history for a while. That provides one with the European background on Christianity. We don't need to research much or look for it; it is part of our DNA. One can then either become a deeply religious person or turn away from it. In any case, this is our base, our culture.

R: But the dimension in which von Bingen lives her faith has to be worked out by any person studying her.

MvT: I started with the assumption that her stance was a natural one. Faith and knowledge were one and the same in the Middle Ages. One did not question faith. When a person has faith today, another person always asks whether you have any doubts. That did not exist back then. During the Middle Ages, religion was the foundation of existence. One believed in God, one believed in the devil, one believed in angels, one believed in paradise, one believed in damnation, in good and bad. In the same way we have faith in our technology today. It exists; it is present. Technological gadgets are lying on our table and we speak into them. Faith was truth. That was my starting point. One did not question anything, the way we do in modern life.

R: You are right; back then one even believed that one lived on a disc . . .

MvT: Yes, today nobody understands that anymore either: how was it possible for the people to believe that the earth is a flat object? Below [the disc] was hell, above it God. And when they all look up, then God was truly there. We still look up and we know that God is not there. If God is anywhere, then he is everywhere.

R: Did you try out different things when visualizing *Vision*?

MvT: It was my wish to get Barbara Sukowa's husband, Robert Longo, a fantastic video artist and painter, to join the project. I wanted him to create [von Bingen's] vision. I wanted a person who would add an entirely different language to the project. But we didn't have the finances to do that. Next, I wanted to do it myself, but then I didn't believe in myself enough to pull it off. Books from the time period visualize Hildegard von Bingen's visions with pictures. But that is so far removed, it would have been tacky.[3] Because of this, I restricted myself to her very first vision that she described herself: a lightning strike came from the heaven and a voice said, "describe what I say to you." We only visualized the heaven, the way it opened up, showing the dazzling beam. That was the starting point. Everything that von Bingen sees thereafter are fantastical, unbelievable images. I would need to be Steven Spielberg and have the possibility of CGI to make this moment more appealing. But finances did not permit that.

R: Overall, the sets appear costly . . .

MvT: I am glad you see it that way (*laughs*). I had a fabulous stage set designer who researched a lot. Also, the [female] props manager[4] brought a lot of passion to the project. They [the crew] all put in tremendous amounts of effort, worked very carefully and researched a lot. My entire team was comprised of people who had never worked on anything related to the Middle Ages prior to this project. Now, they were confronted with questions: "What did cakes look like in the Middle Ages?" Glass did not exist in its modern version back then either; so what did that look like? To explore those matters was a lot of fun; I thought that was really wonderful.

R: What is the reason that we have an increased desire for spirituality in current times? If you think about how many people walk "The Way of St. James."[5]

MvT: Well, Hildegard von Bingen said that spirit and body belong together. She held the idea of a "whole." Pilgrims test their physical endurance in order to encounter a spiritual experience. These experiences merge body and spirit. That's exactly what we gave up over the course of several centuries. The spirit moved further away from the body. Fitness fanatics also move further away from uniting their bodies and spirit as they only train their muscles. Suddenly, walking the Camino, everything is united once again.

R: Did you walk the way?

MvT: No, but I do believe that it is a special experience. Especially during the current crisis, the climate change, the financial catastrophe. Everything that you worked for and built is suddenly gone. So many people suddenly lost their homes and their savings. It's bearable in Germany, but it's especially bad in America. What remains for us besides a spiritual dimension? Many "financial sharks" commit suicide these days. Do they have to commit suicide because they lost their savings? Don't they have something else that they can rebuild their lives on? It's crazy. I can't quite follow their actions.

R: Perhaps it is the feeling of guilt, as they lost other people's money.

MvT: Well, yes, Madoff could have committed suicide; I wouldn't mind, but he is precisely the one not taking that step (*laughs*). He is starting to believe in the afterlife.

R: Were you never intrigued to make a film about male characters?

MvT: I would be intrigued, but men ensure that they make those films. I view it as my task to search a bit. Ironically, men are never asked this question. Or have you ever asked a man whether he wouldn't be intrigued to make a movie about a strong, powerful woman? I'm the only one who gets asked that question.

R: Well, with more equality, maybe in thirty years, would you perhaps [make a movie about men at that point]?

MvT: Men are featured in my films. My films are not void of them. Heino Ferch does an excellent job as Volmar.[6] Especially as he is known for playing a macho.

R: Many thanks for this conversation.

Notes

1. This is a direct translation from the German idiom "Kräuternonne" that von Trotta uses. At the time, nuns produced their own herbs for consumption in fields next to the monasteries.

2. "Diakonie" is derived from the Greek word for "service." In this context, it applies to the work of Christians, who believe that besides worship and preaching, service to one's neighbors is also part of one's active faith in life. It can be viewed as a sister to missionary work.

3. The German word used by von Trotta is "kitsch."

4. The German word for this job is "Requisiteurin."

5. "The Way of St. James," also known as the Camino de Santiago, is an old pilgrimage route, mostly located in Spain that terminates at the Cathedral in Santiago de Compostela. It was one of the most important Christian pilgrimages during the Middle Ages.

6. Heino Ferch portrays Monk Volmar in *Vision*.

"During the Sixties, I Basically Lived as If I Were in the Middle Ages"

Ralf Krämer / 2009

From *Planet Interview*, September 29, 2009. Translated by Monika Raesch. Reprinted by permission of *Planet Interview*.

Margarethe von Trotta speaks about Hildegard von Bingen, herbal remedies, artistic and polytheistic visions, and her ex-husband Volker Schlöndorff.

Ralf Krämer: Ms. von Trotta, did your intense study of Hildegard von Bingen impact your relationship with your primary care physician?
Margarethe von Trotta: No. But since Hildegard von Bingen is well known for her writings about natural remedies, I once tagged along with a "woodsman" who gave classes about herbs.[1] I can now recognize a yarrow. But I don't have any further knowledge.

K: Do you rather trust scientific medicine?
vT: I relate to both. If you have cancer, you should engage scientific medicine and not attempt to save your life by using herbs. I experienced this situation twice with girlfriends who only trusted natural remedies; they both passed away. There is a point beyond which natural remedies are not helpful. I believe that Hildegard would not have anything against medical science today—she was always curious and desired knowledge. Today, she wouldn't be a woman collecting herbs, but would be knowledgeable about physics and modern medicine.[2]

K: How did you persuade your producers to finance a film about Hildegard von Bingen?
vT: I didn't have to do that. This time around, the producers approached me. I already had had the idea of making a movie about her in the 1980s. But back then political cinema was popular. I figured that the type of movie I envisioned was of

no interest to anybody and dropped the idea. A little while ago, I wanted to write a screenplay about Hannah Arendt with my producer, Markus Zimmer. He didn't want that, but said: you once told me about Hildegard von Bingen. Why don't you make a movie about her. And I replied: "Well, sure; if you pay me, I will write that screenplay." I had written the screenplay for Hannah Arendt without receiving any payment.

K: What fascinates you about this nun who lived in the twelfth century?
vT: Her versatility. The way she tries to live out all her talents. That wasn't easy for a woman back then. Of course, her deep faith played a large role; one can't question that factor. During the Middle Ages, one believed in heaven, God, hell, Satan, and damnation. They also believed that the earth is shaped like a disc and hell is located underneath us. One has to remind oneself of those belief systems today [before passing any judgment].

K: Different to other believers, von Bingen believed that she was a chosen one by God . . .
vT: It was rather courageous of her to say: "I have visions." She could have ended up at Satan's doorstep. If the church had damned her, had excommunicated her, that would have been like death, like damnation for the rest of your life on earth. Since her visions were officially acknowledged, she was able to justify building a monastery with and for other nuns. She used her faith, to live out her talents. I think that is genius, the way her subconscious/unconscious guided her actions.

K: People also often speak of film directors having visions that they want to realize. Do you feel a sort of relationship exists between the two situations?
vT: Every director, especially those who also wrote the screenplay, have a vision that he/she wants to realize. The director has to find producers willing to finance the film. There are parallels. Beyond that, such a vision can be a utopia for a better, fairer tomorrow. Once I directed a film about Rosa Luxemburg. Both Rosa and Hildegard repeatedly stood up against those in power and against greed. That is rather modern. Currently, times are darkening, and everybody is focused on enriching oneself. One can quote what both these women have said, and it fully applies today.

K: Could you fulfill your visions of being the director of this film?
vT: Well, the vision was that I can bring something to realization. That is why in France the director is called "réalisateur." If I had turned out to be the way I imagined . . . let's not go there. I still make films. But I did not turn out to be Ingmar Bergman. He was my role model.

K: Do Hildegard von Bingen's visions of God speak to you?

vT: I was a little scared. The first vision had to be translated into the visual world of filmmaking; you couldn't get around that. In that vision, Hildegard gets the order from the lively light to share her knowledge, to not keep it to herself. She was asked to admonish the people and to bring them back to God. I had planned to shoot several visions, but then I realized that I would need a video artist for those, to make them into something new.

K: I meant the question differently: Do you believe that von Bingen truly received her visions from God?

vT: I believe that she was convinced that her visions are messages from God. Personally, I can't imagine that God selects somebody and says to that person: "It is your duty to share the belief with others." If you really believed in a God, then this God would not only be a God for the Christians, but for all faiths. Her visions are only related to Christianity and the Bible. For me, that is a clear pointer that she didn't receive her visions from God. I don't believe that.

K: Would you describe yourself as a believer?

vT: How should I answer that? I only go to church to light candles for sick friends or to find a moment of stillness, whenever there is nobody else there, or hardly anybody. But I don't attend church services. I may be a believing atheist.

K: You represent Hildegard von Bingen as an egoist as well.

vT: That she is an egoist, is an accusation that comes from the others. When the young sister Richardis wants to leave the order, Bingen does behave in a very egoistical manner. Her emotions get the better of her, but that makes her human as well.

K: What are some common features that Hildegard von Bingen shares with the other women that you portray in your films?

vT: I like to look at women who have an idea of what they want to achieve. In the movies, I usually focus on women, but in real life I also look at men. This is not necessarily the result of the success of a person; rather, it is dependent on what one feels and wants to share. When someone moves something from being a thought to realization, that is what I find interesting.

K: Do you feel comfortable in your role as female director who has been reduced to making "women's movies"?

vT: Well, by now it has become something of a brand. It is no longer even a choice. It always approached me like that; at some point, I accepted it.

K: You started in the business as an actress. Why did you never return to acting after you became a director?

vT: Directing was the position I had wished for from the start. Becoming an actress was a detour to becoming a director. I was in France in the early sixties. At that time, filmmakers were cinephiles and, for the first time, directors really got attention. In Germany, actors were the ones with status at the start; nobody paid attention to the directors. The very first movies I saw were by Bergman, Hitchcock, and part of the Nouvelle Vague movement. I thought: "My God, to be able to do this one day would be the best."

K: In France, female Agnès Varda belongs to the predecessor of Nouvelle Vague.

vT: But in Germany, this was not imaginable yet, that somebody like me can direct movies. The New German Cinema did not start until '65/'66 with the movies by Volker Schlöndorff and Alexander Kluge. Unconsciously, I turned towards acting, basically positioned myself at the starting line until the moment arrived when I could sprint over to the directing chair. That was in 1977. And I have not acted ever since. I didn't want to anymore anyway.

K: The unconscious is the reason for you turning your dreams into reality—that is the same way you described Hildegard von Bingen's calling earlier in this interview.

vT: Well, I only see a few parallels, if at all. But if I look at my position as being a woman in the 1960s, you could basically say that I also lived in the Middle Ages; that you can compare. I didn't stand a chance as a woman. But then I chose the way [towards directing] via acting and not via God. (*laughs*) My female colleagues Helke Sander and Helma Sanders-Brahms already directed movies before I did. I sort of arrived a little later.[3]

K: Could one say that you educated yourself as a director by being an actress on movie sets?

vT: I looked at my directors to see how they do it. But Claude Chabrol always just said: "Suprenez moi"—surprise me. And that is difficult, to surprise such a master of his craft. Wolfgang Staude had already become a bit tired [of the profession]; he no longer had a lot of interest. But he appreciated that I knew so much. We discussed film history and he said: "Well, let's continue work. You are going to walk from the right towards the left!" (*laughs*)

K: Do female directors produce different cinema than men do?

vT: Not necessarily. Kathryn Bigelow produced rather manly cinema. In the past, I always fought this question; in the same way as I am fighting this one: "Why do you always make movies about women?" I reply: "If you ask Wim Wenders why he makes movies about men—in the mean time that has changed—then you can ask me that question."

K: In a few weeks, *Pope Joan*[4] will come to theaters, which is another movie about a strong woman from the early Middle Ages. Originally, Volker Schlöndorff, with whom you were married for several years, was supposed to direct the film. Was your interest in Hildegard von Bingen similar to that of Schlöndorff in "the female pope"?
vT: *Pope Joan* is a big spectacle with a budget of EUR 20 million. That is entirely different to my EUR 5 million project, or however much my budget was.

K: One can shoot many spectacles, but this subject is special . . .
vT: When he started that project, mine was still up in the air. But he remembered my first ideas about a Bingen project, and that I owned all the books about her. He spent a lot of time familiarizing himself with Bingen, as preparation for *The Female Pope*. But "the female pope" is an imaginary character, meaning one has a lot of freedom telling the story.

K: How important was Volker Schlöndorff for your career?
vT: Very important. Together with him, I co-directed *The Lost Honor of Katharina Blum*. In the end, I spent more time in the editing room than he did.

K: Did you read his recently published biography?
vT: I have to admit that I haven't finished it yet. He handed me the manuscript, but I was busy with *Vision* and didn't want to look at anything that may put a strain on my focus. And I was certain that I would react rather allergic to some things he had written. I didn't want that in that moment. I was puzzled when he said: "I'm writing my biography," as I always had a much better memory than him; I always had to help him remember things. The book must really be good, given the things I have read about it. But I am certain that many things are incorrect. (*laughs*) He said: "Well, eventually you will write your own biography. Then you can correct all those things."

K: And? Will you do that?
vT: No; why should I? Perhaps if I turn one hundred years old.

K: The latest edition of the feminist journal *Missy* features a survey on the topic: when was the last time you felt disadvantaged based on your gender? I would like to end the interview with this question.

vT: I can't think of anything off the top of my head. Certainly, much remains to be criticized. But those things, such as different salaries for men and women, I denounced those things so often, others should take over my lead. Others follow who scream about those matters. At the moment, I feel content in this world. Perhaps because I am still alive.

Notes

1. Von Trotta used the German word "Waldmensch" in the original interview; its literal translation is "woodsman." Some translators would translate the word as the idiom "crunchy granola," though it is questionable whether von Trotta would have used that term with its specific undertone.

2. Von Trotta used the German word "Kraeuterliese" in the original interview; no equivalent idiom exists in the English language.

3. Von Trotta's own words are "Ich bin da so ein bisschen nachgetroepfelt," a German idiom without equivalent translation.

4. *Pope Joan* (2009), directed by Sönke Wortmann. German title, "Die Päpstin"; direct translation: "The Female Pope."

"Resistance Made Me Mentally Strong"

Petra Ahne and Rudolf Novotny / 2013

From *Frankfurter Rundschau*, January 8, 2013. Translated by Monika Raesch.
Reprinted by permission of *Frankfurter Rundschau*.

Born out of wedlock, when this was still unacceptable, she became a film director, at a time when only men controlled that profession. This is a conversation with Margarethe von Trotta about independence, good relationships, and questions that only women are ever asked.

The Suite in the Grand Hyatt Hotel in Berlin is untouched—Margarethe von Trotta only gives interviews here; she rather stays overnight at her friend's place in Charlottenburg. The director who herself has been residing in Paris for many years is visiting Berlin to introduce *Hannah Arendt*, her film about the German philosopher. Everything in the hotel room is designed in creamy white and dark brown colors—communicating a cold elegance; the only hint of life flows from a colorful fruit basket situated on the table. Until Margarethe von Trotta enters. Clear voice, strong handshake, looking straight at you, at first with an amused expression.

FR: Ms. von Trotta, we would like to talk with you about women.
MvT: Noooo, I don't feel like doing that. Couldn't we talk about Hannah Arendt instead?

FR: Of course, but Hannah Arendt is also a woman and . . .
MvT: I can't listen to this anymore. Everybody wants to know why I showcase strong women [on the screen]. Why do you all ask me this question? And the women I portray are not only strong, they also have their vulnerable areas. This is what it always sounds like: the heroines! Have you ever asked a man why he portrays strong men [on the screen]? I bet you haven't.

FR: Perhaps your women are more complex than most male heroes.

MvT: Aha! Now you attempt this angle! But I know what you are doing! Additionally, these men are not always one-dimensional characters; just look at the most recent James Bond film.

FR: We don't want to ask you why you make movies about women. But one can't but notice that you do—we have the women in the *Rosenstrasse* who fight for their deported men; Rosa Luxemburg; Hildegard von Bingen; and now Hannah Arendt.

MvT: Yes, because Hannah Arendt was an important thinker of the past century. It is a fact, that there were not many female philosophers and political thinkers at that time. If you then select one of these women, it appears to be a feminist statement. Of course, I associate with that. But I don't want to be reduced to that. However, that has happened ever since I started making movies. And now, I reply to those kinds of questions as a women's libber: noooo, you only have the right to ask me questions that you would also ask male directors. And that does not only apply to my film's themes. I'm seventy years old; that is public record; I turned seventy last year. If one's lucky, everybody will celebrate that birthday. But to then tell me that I turned seventy and whether I'm thinking of retiring from the profession—do you really think one would have asked Peter Zadek or Ken Loach that question? In two years, Woody Allen turns eighty. One would never ask him, "Don't you want to retire?" Why do people ask me this question?

FR: Why?

MvT: Because one doesn't have respect for a woman; that's why.

Against All Resistance

FR: But we didn't want to ask you this question either. Instead, we wanted to talk about what has changed for women [over the past decades]. You still had to overcome resistance to become a movie director. Your name was entirely omitted from the credits of *The Lost Honor of Katharina Blum*, even though you co-directed it with Volker Schlöndorff.

MvT: That's okay; I can talk about that.

FR: Would you prefer to be a young female director today?

MvT: This is difficult to answer. Not having it easy made me strong. The higher the resistance, the stronger one becomes. I'm not sure I would still make movies today, if everything would have been easy.

FR: What is different today?

MvT: Today, approximately 50 percent of movies are made by women. That doesn't mean that we have reached the moment where this is a given. Just look at the most recent Cannes Film Festival; no woman was part of the program. Twenty-two films made by twenty-two men. French female directors wrote a letter in protest. Men don't realize when women are omitted. Women have pushed though enough that we are able to make movies, although we receive lower budgets than men. I'm not sure a woman would have received the 100 million [unclear what denominations von Trotta refers to] that Tom Tykwer was just given to make *Cloud Atlas*. My female producer says that when she submits a script by a female director, that it has a higher chance of rejection than the script of a male director. My producer is not a feminist; she simply is a successful forty-year-old; she doesn't need to go the extra mile to be acknowledged and to be taken seriously. But she noticed the treatment of female director's work.

FR: Men still dominate many areas.

MvT: Yes, I just read about a young woman who endeavors to open more doors for women in higher positions of power. In those positions where you usually only have men. She says that women often don't want these jobs in which one has power over others. It is the norm for men. To be powerful is the norm for men. Women step back, and not because they don't believe in themselves, but because they don't value the behavior that men exhibit and don't want to alter their own behavior. This type of fight is something that men are better at. I would be concerned about developing a poor personality.

FR: Does the reason for this lie with the corporate culture developed by men, or do women seek power less?

MvT: Many women would contradict you; and one can't generalize—but I do think that many women do not desire the power and fights that accompany it. For men, it's almost a sexual act.

FR: At the same time, many things between the sexes have changed. Many young fathers, for instance, do take care of their kids.

MvT: I am always happy to see that, men sitting on playgrounds. I see this in Paris, where I live. That didn't happen when I had a young child. When I went to the playground with my son, only women would sit on the benches; they would crochet; and that was annoying. I like that things have equalized. That a man's attitude has changed, no longer feeling ashamed to take care of kids.

FR: You lived in Paris for the first time as an au pair when you were eighteen. Why in Paris?

MvT: At the time, many young women did that as we did not feel comfortable living in Germany under then-chancellor Konrad Adenauer. We wanted to see the world. For instance, at the same time as I was an au pair, Jutta Brueckner, Ula Stroeckl, and Janna Schygulla—who would become directors as well—were also in Paris. We didn't know each other then. America was too far away; Paris was accessible by car.

As Hitchhiker on the Road

FR: You traveled by flagging cars down? Your mom must have figuratively died from being scared.

MvT: Of course, I never told her that. And I didn't do it all the time, but sometimes it was the only option. I remember one trip especially; I wanted to return from Paris to Düsseldorf. I was stateless until my first marriage, like Hannah Arendt, and I needed a visa for every country. I sat on the train without the visa to travel through Belgium; you had to pay for those papers; that was too expensive. I thought—I can cheat my way through the country—but I was removed from the train in the middle of the night by a border guard. I returned to Paris by flagging down a car. Of course, this was not without its dangers. Men even asked whether I wasn't scared traveling like that by myself, asking whether I had been assaulted? My answer was always the same: no, never. That meant, of course, the guy asking me the question now couldn't be the first one.

FR: Did you find in Paris what you had been looking for in your life?

MvT: Yes, I discovered the power of film. I watched movies by Ingmar Bergman, Hitchcock, all of the Nouvelle Vague. That was at the beginning of the sixties; Germans were watching "Heimatfilme"/homeland-films.[1] For my mother and me, film was an art form; same as the theatre, opera, exhibits, concerts. In Paris, I started to make movies with French students, including one proper feature-length picture. They managed to save enough time to do that. It was a philosophically extreme thriller. It never made it to the cinemas, but it wasn't bad either. I still own a copy. The director was my back-then boyfriend; he worshipped Orson Welles. A second feature was being planned with me as the main protagonist. I thought, in that case I do need a bit of formal training. I returned to Germany, studied, and took acting lessons on the side. In the end, the film was never made. I remained in Germany and became an actress. But in the end, that was a detour.

FR: You left as a good au pair-girl and returned as an actress?

MvT: I wasn't just an au pair, I also studied. I financed my life being an au pair.

FR: Your mom had not hoped that you would become an actress?

MvT: I was always permitted to do what I wanted. My mother was very tolerant.

She trusted me, and I never went behind her back. Yes, she never knew about me flagging down cars; she would have been too scared. In the big picture, I always told her everything. I was also given more freedom than my girlfriends. They had a 10:00 p.m. curfew; I didn't have one. My girlfriends, my God, some of them really tortured themselves.

FR: How much of an impact did it have on you being a child born out of wedlock and being raised by a single mom at a time when that was looked down upon?
MvT: Of course, that was held against me quite often: out of wedlock, stateless. There were a few things that a good citizen and a proper country did not appreciate much. But the more one gets attacked, the stronger one becomes. Given that I was always the best student in class, nobody could really get to me. I helped everybody with their homework; I permitted them to cheat off of me. That was my defense mechanism.

FR: Would you have preferred to be more like the other children?
MvT: Being stateless was annoying. I was stateless and only owned what was referred to as a "Fremdenpass" [a foreign passport]. Just this word in itself says it all: I was a foreigner. I think I only got married for the first time to gain citizenship. I didn't have the desire to be married. Not at all. But [being stateless] was a real reason. And since my husband really wanted to get married—well, then let's do so. I didn't force him to marry me. I never forced anybody to marry me. There is the saying that it is always the women who want to get married. I can't confirm that.

FR: Your second husband, Volker Schlöndorff, also had a stronger desire to marry you than vice versa?
MvT: He had to persuade me for one year until I agreed. But this is the way it is when one wants to hold on and keep somebody; one thinks: if I marry her, it will be harder for her to leave. He also said: you were already married once before; it is not as important for you anymore. But it is the first time for me, and I would like to get married.

FR: You have been separated for a long time. Was it difficult for you to be an equal to a man given your desire for self-realization?
MvT: Of course. I live alone. It is often difficult for men to stand next to strong women. I felt that a lot when I was younger. Men said, that we are feminists and desire gender equality. And then you checked out how they lived in their personal lives, and you realized they were not that progressive. They wanted the role of the women to remain what it always had been. I experienced this a lot. Especially with the liberals. I enjoy being on my own. I am not standing in this world by myself. I

have a son. I lived together with men for long enough. Everything you can experience with men, I have experienced.

FR: What would your ideal partnership be like?

MvT: Mutual support to explore one's talents and to live life to the fullest. To provide one another with courage and assist the other to seize opportunities that present themselves. Hannah Arendt and Heinrich Blücher had such a supportive relationship.

FR: In your movie, you portray the relationship that has lasted for twenty-five years already as very close and caring. When she sees her husband, her face always lights up like that of a girl deeply in love.

MvT: The two of them could also argue very intensely; they screamed at one another. And he was a womanizer; he had girlfriends. But they had a common understanding and tolerance: to acknowledge the other as the person they are; and this led to deep spiritual exchanges. Add to that that the other represented a piece of home, meaning, we represented what was left of Germany, besides the language. When they met in 1936 in exile in Paris, they began to think and consider the world together. And they hid together. They truly did not have any papers; I did have a passport. But my mom was in the same situation as they were: when she fled Moscow—the kingdom of the Czars—she did not have any identification papers either. A Norwegian diplomat invented a pass for these people, the foreigners' passport. That permitted them to at least have some form of identification: one was still stateless but one's existence was documented. But these emigrants did not even have that. There are a few books by Erich Maria Remarque that describe this time of the emigrants in Pairs. They are worth a read.

FR: Many people "break" when reading Remarque. What carries one through all of it?

MvT: Attitude, intellect, education. Those can help. On the other hand, Walter Benjamin eventually committed suicide, after his failed attempt to flee to Portugal. At that moment, he had no inner drive left; he didn't want [to suffer] any longer. Of course, there are people who did not make it through [this very difficult time].

Minted by Hannah Arendt

FR: Hannah Arendt's strength is the theme of your film. You narrate how she observes the judicial process of Nazi criminal Adolf Eichmann in Israel. She bears being made a dangerous enemy due to her perspective that Eichmann is not a monster, but a simple bureaucrat. Where did this strength originate in her?

MvT: She received it from her mother who raised her. Her father died when she was eight years old. Her mother was a liberal thinker, highly educated, and viewed Rosa Luxemburg as a role model. Hannah Arendt was treated like an adult at an early age. People had confidence in her, and her mother supported her a lot.

FR: The film is set at the beginning of the 1960s. At this moment, Hannah Arendt lives as a recognized philosopher in New York. But she is also a woman in a world filled with men at the time. How much did that impact her own thought processes?
MvT: She was mostly influenced by Martin Heidegger. Everybody rushed to him and his notions at the time. He was the secret king of thinking. All young people who wanted to study philosophy at the time and were seeking out a new way of thinking turned to Heidegger. These were mostly men. But Arendt was so brilliant from the very beginning that she never had the issue of male/female inequality or competition. She also looked very pretty. If you see a picture of Hannah Arendt at the age of eighteen—she was beautiful. As a result, she was worshipped by her male colleagues.

FR: In your film, the male colleagues say: "Hannah Arendt, a pretty arrogant woman with little emotion . . ."
MvT: That's what women are reproached with when they are very intelligent and [dare to] show their intelligence. I mean she never hid that she was more intelligent than others. To lower her status, she is being demeaned in that manner ["Dann wird sie eben auf diese Weise abgekanzelt"]. You can't say that she is stupid or that she isn't knowledgable. Instead, you say: she is unfeeling and arrogant.

FR: In the film, you can literally watch Hannah Arendt think: she observes Adolf Eichmann during the judicial proceedings, and one can feel how she develops her own attitude of and towards him. Not many people manage to trust in themselves when they have an opinion that nobody else shares.
MvT: I think she developed her independence so strongly when she was forced to leave Germany in 1933. First, she mostly lived in philosophy. As an emigrant, she saw the larger world for the first time and realized what was happening. She had to adjust her behavior accordingly. Her husband, Heinrich Blücher, was an independent thinker. He was a representative of the proletariat who educated himself. Both of them taught each other a lot. The big argument that Hannah Arendt makes is: would I still want to live with myself in this world, if I were to behave differently? I really like that thought. You don't have a law or somebody else who tells you in which way to think and act. Of course, that could also happen unconsciously. During Nazism, many simple people helped out others. For the most part, mostly simple people hid the Jews. You don't need much intellect for

that. It was a feeling: you can't act in any other way. Maybe not all people have that feeling. Many, many could live with themselves very well [not helping another].

FR: Why do you show original archival footage of the Eichmann trial in your film?
MvT: I knew that I would do this from the very start of the project. To understand Hannah Arendt's analysis of Eichmann, one had to see the real man himself. If I would have cast an actor for the role, people would have simply said: man, he is good. One would only have seen the actor's brilliant performance, but not the mediocrity of the actual man.

FR: What was the film's reception in Israel where Hannah Arendt is still a controversial figure?
MvT: Her book about the judicial proceedings was first published in Israel in 2002. In the United States and in Germany it was already published in 1963. That alone tells us how much the country was fighting [her thoughts]. The film had a surprisingly positive reception. I expected more opposition. But it played at a women's film festival; the proper premiere is not until April.

FR: A women's film festival?
MvT: Yes, they showed an entire retrospective of my work. I had agreed to come as the country-wide premiere of *Hannah Arendt* was supposed to happen at the same time. I don't attend every single women's film festival anymore; that time has passed. But then the premiere was moved on short notice to April; I wasn't able to cancel the film festival anymore at that point. I had a good time. The women were very intelligent and modern [in their way of thinking].

FR: Now we have spoken a lot about women after all.
MvT: Yes, and that's okay. I don't take all of this so serious anymore. That's the good thing about getting older: one isn't as radical anymore.

Notes

1. "Heimtfilme," translated as "homeland-films," was a genre popular in Germany, Austria, and Switzerland from the 1940s to the 1970s. Possibly the most important convention was presence of the outdoors; films were usually shot in the Alps, the Black Forest, or the Lüneburg Heath.

Thinking without a Railing

Oliver Heilwagen / 2013

From *Kunst und Film*, January 9, 2013. Translated by Monika Raesch. Reprinted by permission of Oliver Heilwagen.

The film *Hannah Arendt* focuses on the hypotheses of the philosopher Hannah Arendt in regards to the Eichmann Trial. In this interview, director von Trotta discusses some biographical parallels between Arendt and herself as well as three variances on the concepts of thinking and seduction.

Oliver Heilwagen: Mrs. von Trotta, how did you get the idea to make a movie about Hannah Arendt?

Margarethe von Trotta: I read a lot about Jewish history when I made the 2003 film *Rosenstrasse*. I read about German women who protested their Jewish husbands' incarcerations in a Nazi prison in 1943. Part of that material was also Arendt's book about the "Eichmann Trial." I was particularly interested in those chapters in which she described how individual European countries treated Jews: whether they were handed over to the Nazis (or not).

Following that, a friend of mine "demanded" that I make a movie about Hannah Arendt. I was not convinced but hesitated: I asked my scriptwriter Pamela Katz—she wrote the script for *Rosenstrasse*—and she liked the idea. My friend and Pamela cornered me until I relented and agreed.

OH: What side of Hannah Arendt interested you the most: the philosopher or the political thinker (who focused intensely on Jews)?

MvT: Hannah Arendt's background was academic philosophy. Her eyes were opened only through her own experiences of having to flee, having to emigrate, and related to that feel abandoned, and meeting her future husband Heinrich Blücher—who was an anarchist and member of the communist "Spartakusbund." Basically, she fell into reality.

MvT: She slowly moved out of the discrepancy she found herself in that was the result of her idealist thinking and the dark reality she was experiencing. Nonetheless, she never stopped being a philosopher; her last books took a philosophical approach to some extent. For me, two quotes of hers are of particular importance: "I want to understand" and "Thinking without a railing."[1]

Additionally, you have some matches in our biographies: she was stateless; I was as well until my first marriage. She described this feeling of being foreign with the following words: "We evolved into strange people,[2] into new human creatures: our enemies plugged us into concentration camps; our friends plugged us into internment camps."[3]

She only felt that the German language and culture was her home; otherwise she was stateless. I could relate to that. Such commonalities in one's biographies provide the energy to be genuinely interested in another person.

OH: Some co-producers did not view Barbara Sukowa as the best actress to take on the role of Hannah Arendt. Why?

MvT: I don't understand that either; some people don't have an imagination. They ask: Sukowa is blond and has blue eyes—how can she portray a Jew? She already proved as the character Rosa Luxemburg that she is capable of that—even with blue eyes.

I think the other way around: if an actor or actress looks similar to the character they are supposed to play, audiences will be distracted [by those similarities]. They will be pondering whether the actor/actress is truly similar to the actual person. If I instead take the approach and claim: this person is taking on the role, the audience is more open to arguments the character/narrative is going to make—and that is what's important to me.

OH: How did you get the idea to focus the film on the three to four years of the Eichmann controversy?

MvT: That idea emerged slowly. At first, we tried to adapt her entire life in a traditional film format. That would have resulted in a rushed narrative, constantly heading from one key moment in her life to the next without having the time to create any depth, to explain what any of these moments mean, and to show what it means to think.[4]

Arendt's friend Mary McCarthy described Arendt's approach to thinking very nicely: she lay on a couch with open eyes; you were not permitted to speak to her. This scene repeats itself numerous times throughout the film. It is these quiet and calm moments that turned her into such an energetic fighter.

OH: One key element of her [Arendt's] theory of totalitarianism is omitted in the film: the parallels between Fascism and Stalinism as forms of reigning [a country] and how they differ from others.

MvT: You cannot make a movie about a book. You need an enemy to make a movie: you have Arendt on the one side, Eichmann is positioned on the other. He is a completely mediocre man who does not manage to form one correct sentence. She looks at him, and he has no idea that she will use him to formulate an example of the banality of evil. This will forever remain attached to his name. Would he have known this, perhaps he would have been proud. She fights with him as an enemy, as she is forced to recognize and describe him.

Heidegger is situated in between the two—she views him as the "secret king of thinking"; that's what she called him. He could think, but nonetheless supported Nazism. The movie points out three versions: carelessness, seductive thinking, and thinking without seduction.

OH: The film provides a critical depiction of Israel; for instance, in one scene, we see Hannah Arendt being intimidated by Israeli secret service forces. What was Israel's reaction to your film?

MvT: I don't know that yet. It received positive critiques at a women's festival, but it won't be released in Israel until April. At that moment, I am expecting some negative criticism. Arendt's book, *Eichmann in Jerusalem*, was first published in Israel in 2002; that means, forty years after she wrote it. On the other hand, several Israel film houses participated in the production of my film.

OH: What question would you ask Arendt if you were given the chance?

MvT: If she is okay with the film and the way I chose to portray her life in the film. I would love to hear from her: yes, you understand me.

Notes

1. In German, Arendt's direct quotes were "Ich will verstehen" and "Denken ohne Geländer," the latter also having been selected as the title of the interview by interviewer Oliver Heilwagen. In journalist Gregory Smulewixz-Zucker's article *In Conversation* for the *Brooklyn Rail*, "Geländer" has been translated as "banister." It is unclear whether the filmmaker used the word herself during the interview for the magazine or whether the interviewer translated it himself. This interview can also be found in this volume.

2. Arendt uses the word "Gestalten."

3. Arendt uses the word "Internierungslager."

4. As von Trotta speaks in allegories that don't translate directly into English, her original statement is provided here: "Das waere aber ein Ritt ueber den Bodensee geworden; von einer Station zur naechsten, ohne die Zeit, ein Thema zu vertiefen zu koennen und zu zeigen, was es eigentlich bedeutet, zu denken."

Interview with Margarethe von Trotta on Her Film *Hannah Arendt*

Stéphane Humber / 2013

From *Cinéalliance*, April 21, 2013. Translated by M. A. Salvodon. Reprinted by permission of Stéphane Humber and Gérard Chargé.

We are presenting the interview with the filmmaker Margarethe von Trotta for her film *Hannah Arendt* that will come out in theatres April 24, 2013. This interview was conducted during the "17èmes Rencontres du Cinéma de Gérardmer."

Cinéalliance: How did you learn about Hannah Arendt's story?
Margarethe von Trotta: I read all about the history of Judaism, the history of Israel, the history of German Jews, and I read her book on Adolf Eichmann and the banality of evil. She not only describes the trial but she also describes how different countries reacted to Germany's request to hand over its Jews during the war.

At that moment, I had not yet thought of making a film.

C: And what do you think of the ensuing controversy?
MvT: Two criticisms were made. One: Arendt didn't see Eichmann as Satan, a diabolical man as others saw him. Two: the five pages that she wrote on Jewish leaders who had been, in fact, too obedient.

C: And what is your opinion on it?
MvT: I don't say that she was correct and that her critics were wrong. I let the viewers judge for themselves.

C: Why did you use real images of the trial from the archives?
MvT: It was very important to me. If I had taken an actor, we would have only seen his talent as an actor by saying that he was good, but I wanted the viewer to see what Hannah Arendt had seen. In this way, the viewer could also tell himself

that Eichmann had been a rather mediocre bureaucrat. And one can only show this with real images.

C: Maurice Papon had the same kind of defense as Adolf Eichmann.
MvT: Yes, if everyone is guilty to a certain extent, then no one is guilty. They stopped feeling guilty.

C: Did you have problems getting financing for the film?
MvT: We were told that the film was not commercial enough when we tried to secure funds in Germany at the beginning.

C: Can you tell us about the diction that the actress Barbara Sukowa had to adopt?
MvT: Barbara Sukowa has been living in New York for twenty years. She speaks English perfectly. On YouTube, she listened to the real Hannah Arendt. Hannah Arendt's accent was very strong. So we wanted to slightly lower her level to avoid making a caricature of it. Three months before filming began, Barbara started to practice her accent with her friends and family. It became natural for her and so the accent doesn't sound artificial on screen.

C: Did you have Barbara Sukowa in mind for this film?
MvT: Yes, I had her in mind, but no one wanted her in Germany because she is blond and has blue eyes. Yes, she played Rosa Luxemburg. I demanded that she play Hannah Arendt and now everyone is happy about it.

C: Why not put images from the camps when she is referring to them in the film?
MvT: That would have been too obvious. I wanted to stay focused on the trial. Now there are many films on the war and on Nazism. It comes in waves. There is a renewed interest in this history. And given what happened, these films are made by people who don't respect each other as human beings.

Margarethe von Trotta and Barbara Sukowa

Sabine Russ / 2013

This interview was commissioned by and first published in *BOMB Daily*, June 13, 2013.
© Bomb Magazine, New Art Publications, and its Contributors. All rights reserved. The
BOMB Digital Archive can be viewed at www.bombmagazine.org. Reprinted by permission.

Since the 1960s, German actress, writer, and film director Margarethe von Trotta
has put out an impressive number of intricate close-up portraits of women—always fervent and independent thinkers, ahead of their era, and determined to
widen their more or less restricted radius of action. Many of von Trotta's films take
place in twentieth-century Germany at critical junctures, in times of repression
and violence, or at the cusp of historic change. *Rosa Luxemburg* (1986) takes us to
the days of the procommunist Spartacus League of 1919; *Marianne and Juliane*
(1981) to the 1970s of the Red Army Faction, Germany's militant extreme left;
Rosenstrasse (2003) to 1943 Berlin and the Holocaust; and *The Other Woman* (2006)
to post-wall Germany coming to terms with its split personalities.

Von Trotta tends to not dwell on illustrating the tense, riotous, or terrifying
streets of an era; she rather zooms in on its human faces. As viewers, what we see
and hear are less the gunfire and the shouts of a time period than the protagonists'
most subtle thoughts, and, often, simply silences. A decisive moment, an instance
of personal or political upheaval might only be reflected in the movement of an
eye or the twitch of a facial muscle. It is this minute detail, this very intimacy
and Hautnähe (closeness to the skin) that make for the human largeness of von
Trotta's films. The psychological acuity she brings to her characters, along with
her inquisitive and unbiased approach to "historicized" figures, are what make her
works so memorable and engrossing. Von Trotta's latest feature, *Hannah Arendt*,
looks again at Germany and its darkest years, but this time from New York and
through the eyes of German Jewish political theorist Hannah Arendt, who fled
her country and found exile in the United States. The film focuses on a distinct
and challenging period in Arendt's life, the years around her coverage of the Adolf

Eichmann trial in 1961 and her theory of the "banality of evil," which resulted in great controversy and affected Arendt's life and work for years to come.

While von Trotta has worked with many exceptional German performers (among them Jutta Lampe, Katja Riemann, Hanna Schygulla, and Maria Schrader), the actor who has appeared most frequently in her films is Barbara Sukowa, who is superb here as a bold, vulnerable, dignified, shaken, and brilliant Hannah Arendt.

Sabine Russ: Barbara, you are based in New York, but Margarethe, you are here from Germany for the official opening of your film *Hannah Arendt* in the United States.

Margarethe von Trotta: Yes. The film was sold in thirty countries—Mexico, Japan . . . and they all want us to come and promote the film. We could go everywhere (only the Arab countries are not interested). This morning I was invited to Santiago, Chile. But we can't go everywhere; we have to go on with filmmaking and not only speak about what we already did.

SR: You two have a long history of working together.

MvT: This is the sixth film we've done together since I cast Barbara in the role of Marianne as Gudrun Ensslin. That was in *Die Bleierne Zeit* (or *Marianne and Juliane*) in 1981. I knew Barbara from the Fassbinder movies.

SR: After making films about several headstrong and unrelenting women like Rosa Luxemburg, the Ensslin sisters, Hildegard von Bingen—all of whom were played by Barbara Sukowa—Hannah Arendt is another quite challenging role.

MvT: Very challenging. I feared Hannah Arendt and it took a long time to make the film. I wrote a part of the script in my relatives' apartment in New York and I had a big portrait of Hannah on the wall—with a cigarette. I used to say to my sister-in-law, "Oh, she is so not friendly with me." (laughter)

Barbara Sukowa: I had the same experience. I had a photo of Hannah on my desk while we were working on the movie. At some point I just had to turn it around—I couldn't stand the way she was looking at me so critically. But now she looks friendly. I think we just projected our fear onto her.

MvT: Lotte Köhler, Arendt's close friend and editor, was very helpful in the process. She told us things that you don't find in Hannah's biographies or in her letters. Lotte was very fond of the idea of Barbara playing Hannah's part. Hannah liked Rosa Luxemburg and Lotte liked the way Barbara played Rosa in the film. When Lotte Köhler died two years ago, just before we started filming, all of a sudden I had the feeling that Hannah Arendt was now with us.

SR: Lotte Köhler released her to you, so to speak?

MvT: Perhaps she went to Hannah and said, "It's okay for them to make a film about you, I know them, you can trust them; they are sympathetic and intelligent."

SR: You have made many memorable films about women who changed the way we look at certain things—among them a twelfth-century saint, a revolutionary terrorist, and a spy for the Stasi. What was it that drew you to the political theorist Hannah Arendt?

MvT: She is one of the most interesting figures of the twentieth century. And after I had done several films about German history of the last century, Hannah Arendt fit in a way that allowed me to speak about something I couldn't speak about before—she is looking back, while Rosa Luxemburg was looking forward. Rosa was full of utopian ideas and hopes and she was imprisoned and in the end murdered. There was a real contradiction between what she was expecting and envisioning and the suffering she endured. Then there were the women in *Rosenstrasse*, they lived through "the dark time," as Hannah described those years. That was really the middle of the century, the Second World War, the Holocaust: the dark time. And then came Hannah Arendt, a German Jew, who experienced and survived this time, and she is looking back, trying to understand it. No one can understand the crimes of the Nazis of course, but she looked back not in anger but asking, "How could they?"

SR: You played Hannah's role so intensely, one could say genuinely. The film shows both the joy and torment of thought, of inquiry.

BS: Yes, that's in the script of course. But as an actress I have to really understand what was going on in her head, or at least I have to imagine what was going on in her head. When I approached her, I first read her books and did a lot of research on her work, on what she was writing about, trying to find out what her position was. The next step was to learn about her personal life, which you find out in letters to her friends and the letters to her husband. So you kind of build that person for yourself. You have to find and entrance for yourself—where do I connect to her?

SR: There were many silent scenes where Arendt is just immersed in thought—a mind rather than a body.

BS: In life I actually have a really hard time hiding my thoughts. People can easily read me—if I'm angry about something, it's visible. Maybe that was good for this role. When I was thinking something it came across. But this also has to do with the way the film is built. There are these spaces of thinking—when Hannah is lying on her couch smoking, or when she's watching Eichmann at the trial. These are the moments where also the audience gets a chance to reflect. There is this quiet space where the viewer is let into the process. No quick editing or music is glued over it.

SR: It is rare in film nowadays to find this slowness and these breathing spaces.
MvT: Arendt's thinking position was to lie down while smoking and looking up to the ceiling. This is an actual description by Mary McCarthy.

SR: How much did Hannah's character change from the script once you started filming?
MvT: We followed the script but Barbara is a thinking person and not obeying a director's orders. She knows exactly what to do.
BS: Of course there's the script but then, when you come onto the set, it's always a different situation. Then you have other actors. That changes and stimulates things. If you are face-to-face with Janet McTeer, something more is triggered in you. For me it's very important to work with good actors, to have somebody to riff off, to respond to. When you are open to that it enhances and changes the role.

SR: In all of Margarethe's films you've played these really potent roles. There is some deep connection between the women you have portrayed; they are all rebels in a way, ahead of their time.
BS: All of them were stepping over some border. They wanted more than was given to them in their time and they were all thinkers. But as an actress I have to make them very differently as people, the way they move their bodies, the way they look out. Hildegard von Bingen, for instance was in a monastery where everything is very quiet around her. So I'm not moving my eyes a lot. Hannah Arendt is much more alert, she has a very different way of looking at people. Hildegard has a more meditative demeanor. This comes all together in the way the movie is filmed, in the costumes and in the set. Rosa was a warm person, she loved plants—
MvT: —and birds.
BS: It's a whole different thing in your body that get's stimulated and triggered by the outside.
MvT: And Rosa Luxemburg also had a physical deficiency, she limped.
BS: There is one thing they all have in common that's really interesting to me— they all had at a very young age, a traumatic experience. Rosa was sick, she spent a year in bed; Hildegard was taken away from her family; and Hannah Arendt lost her father at the age of six. That might have resulted for them in intellectualizing things, fleeing reality, and going into the world of thinking or imagining.

SR: Was this a connection you were conscious of, Margarethe?
MvT: I approached these women as historical figures but it is an unconscious

process too. I think my choices have a lot to do with me, which is normal. You can't escape yourself. The script for *Hannah Arendt* I wrote with Pamela Katz, but *Rosa Luxemburg* and *Vision*, the film about Hildegard von Bingen, I wrote alone, the script is all me. They all had a loss in their childhood but they also searched for something that was not meant for them in their time or went way beyond what their era offered to them. They wanted something that was not then granted to them as women and that is interesting to me.

After every film or Q&A, people come up to me with suggestions—"Here is another female historical figure who is perfect for you. You have to do it." Yesterday, someone said, "I wrote a book about communist resistance in Germany, you should make a film about this woman." They can't imagine that I'm not just making films about women that were important in history. There has to be something more for me and it's also significant that Barbara played them all. I always say to Barbara, "You have to do it"—because there is a line that connects our lives to these women.

SR: Your films don't evaluate or judge these women's paths or their historical circumstances. You don't monumentalize the characters, which would remove them from us. Instead you are bringing them intimately close in a human way. There are achievements and failures in equal measure. They are shown with both vulnerabilities and their strengths.

MvT: None of my characters are portrayed like heroes or put on pedestals. I could have done Rosa Luxemburg as a revolutionary hero but that was not interesting to me. I actually could have done a coproduction with the former GDR. They were eager to step in. But I had a friend, an expert on Rosa Luxemburg in East Germany, who gave me access to a lot of material, among them letters, which were not yet published at the time. But my friend, who was even in the Communist Party, said, "Don't do your film with my country. They will force you to do a pedestal movie, to make Rosa Luxemburg into—"

SR: A bronze statue. That's what she was for us in the East. I grew up in East Germany. There was only one official story of Rosa Luxemburg that seemed eternally written in stone. You made your film in the mid-eighties, before the wall came down.

BS: There was not much material in the West in 1985. We bought our books about Rosa Luxemburg in East Germany.

MvT: And it was my triumph that after the film you could buy books about Rosa Luxemburg in West Germany too. Suddenly the bookstores had her writings, her letters, and so on. Same with the Hannah Arendt film, now you can find her book about the Eichmann trial in the stores. More people are reading Arendt's *Eichmann* *in Jerusalem* than before. Even when it first came out in 1963, it was not as successful as after this film.

SR: How do you feel about historical accuracy—if something like that exists—versus your interpretation of these figures?

MvT: I'm not a historian and I'm not a documentarist. I'm a fiction-maker, even if I'm trying to be true and to be as close as possible to the person I'm describing. But I have the freedom to mix it up. There are some scenes where we put two people in one. For instance, the dialogue when Hannah comes to Jerusalem and her friend Kurt Blumenfeld turns his back to her is from a letter exchange she had with Gershom Scholem. Because Scholem is not in the film, we put his lines in the mouth of Blumenfeld. These are the liberties you can take as a fiction filmmaker compared to a historian. When I describe a person like Hannah, I don't have to come from today's perspective and from what we know about her at this point of take into account the critiques she has gotten on her work—no, as a filmmaker I just go with her. I'm looking with her eyes, describing her with her own eyes. And the people who are criticizing her, they are right there with her in the film. As a spectator you can choose: Am I on her side or on the side of Blumenfeld?

SR: People don't read as much these days but depend more on bits from information networks and on images for their knowledge of history. For many viewers, your film might be their only encounter with a historical figure like Hannah Arendt—

MvT: But I'm not a teacher and I don't want to give lessons to anybody. I'm reading all the time with great pleasure. For me books are like bread, I can't live without them. Hannah Arendt wrote so many things and it's sometimes difficult to understand her. You really have to concentrate. It's not like novels, which you can "digest" much more easily.

In my film, I wanted to give the sensation of the pleasure of thinking, the pleasure of trying to reach the depth of something instead of just flying over it. In the film you get the feeling that Hannah can just go deeper and deeper, that she understands more and more. And if you give the viewers the chance to go with her, they feel the pleasure and the satisfaction too. Not only because of what they have seen but because they made an effort to follow her.

BS: One of my sons, who by no means loves every film I do—I don't think Hildegard von Bingen was on top of his list—came out of *Hannah Arendt* and said, "You know, this is the kind of movie I want to see with my friends and then go out for dinner and talk about it for hours." You say you don't want to teach but your films are invitations to ask questions and to talk.

SR: I read that *Rosenstrasse*—your film about non-Jewish wives standing up for their Jewish husbands who had been imprisoned in a Berlin factory building in 1943, awaiting deportation—stirred up a lot of controversy in Germany. It was said that the events shown in your film didn't really happen that way.

MvT: There was one historian who spoke against the film, saying that the Jews held at Rosenstrasse were not meant to go to Auschwitz. But all the people I spoke with—there were still eyewitnesses, when I made the film in 2003—were convinced that the prisoners were headed for the concentration camps. But even if this weren't the case, the women couldn't know that. In the film you are there with them. The focus is on their protest and on the fact that they had the courage to stand up for their men, their Jewish husbands. They came back day after day and eventually it became a demonstration. It was a strong signal and that was the point of the film.

SR: And another point was to ask, "If such protest was possible, why wasn't there more of it?" What has been your experience with the historians' response in Germany to the Hannah Arendt film?

MvT: There have been some historians who complained about the film not being based on new findings, like, "Now we know that Eichmann was much more intelligent and that he played up a role during the trial."

BS: But it actually doesn't matter, it's about the phenomenon of this type of person. So if he wasn't the obedient bureaucrat he pretended he was, there were hundreds of people who were like that.

MvT: When film critics are not so familiar with a subject, like Hannah Arendt's work, in order to not embarrass themselves, they prefer to have historians write about the film. And then the historians "know it better."

BS: As an actor or director, when you are so involved in your subject, you really know quite a lot about it. And of course if someone is writing a review, you can't expect the writer to know everything. For example, Mary McCarthy had said that Hannah Arendt lecturing was like watching Sarah Bernardt, the great French actress, who was really over the top. But we made a decision to not show her that way in the film. Just recently somebody sent me a review from *Süddeutsche Zeitung* that said I played Hannah way too "pathetisch," meaning exalted, "which Hannah Arendt wasn't." I thought, wait a minute, first of all, she actually was exalted and, second, I actually didn't play her like that.

MvT: I remember the *New York Times* critic writing about *Rosenstrasse*, criticizing that I showed no men protesting on the street. She said I did that because I'm a feminist and only want to show women. But obviously, all the non-Jewish men were at the front, they were soldiers and couldn't have been there. And then she wrote, I only show the Jews as victims while they also had weapons. That negative review really affected the reception of the film in the US.

SR: After getting so close to her life and her thinking, how does Hannah Arendt live on for you?

BS: I'm still reading her. I still try to understand certain things about her. It's strange, when I play a character I really don't know what part stays in me. For me it's kind of over when the film is finished.

SR: I guess you have to make room for the next thing.

BS: I also forget a lot. Some of it is really a pity because I invest so much when I'm working on these roles. It's great to read about the characters and dive into all the material, figure it out, read between the lines, try to get the essence of somebody, try to get the mask off this person, find out what was done for others, what was their real temperature. It would be so nice to have that as a library in my head because for other things it would be good to be able to access these experiences, but then it's like a faint memory.

SR: Maybe it has to be like that.

BS: I should ask Meryl Streep if she has the same problem—after all the characters she has played. (laughter) Some essential stuff stays, some basic facts, but the details are just gone.

SR: For many viewers you will be so identified with these characters you have played. You are almost inseparable. But you just leave them behind.

BS: There were quite a few people who were against my casting as Hannah Arendt.

SR: Why?

BS: Because I really don't look like her. It was even more strange with Rosa Luxemburg. There was all this resistance against my playing her part but eventually people thought Rosa Luxemburg looked like me because there are not so many photos of her.

You know, the older I get the more mysterious acting becomes to me. There are all the things you do, but then there are also all the things you don't do that have something to do with it. Hannah Arendt actually said this one thing, which I thought was so amazing: "You are the least alone when you are all with yourself and when you do nothing the most happens"—or something like that. So there is a lot happening when you don't do anything. I don't know what happens sometimes, it just kind of flows into the performance. It's not something I consciously determine.

MvT: It's like Buddhist meditation. Your brain works the most vividly when you are mediating, when you think of nothing. Scientists measuring brain activity found the least brain activity in couples in love. (laughter)

SR: Was it difficult to get the original footage of the Eichmann trial?

MvT: No, that was easy. It's all in the Steven Spielberg Jewish Film Archive in Jerusalem. Spielberg had bought the entire original video record of the Adolf Eichmann trial. The foundation was very helpful and they gave me the material for not too much money. Also, the Israelis were co-producers; we got subsidized by the state and also by the city of Jerusalem. They were in the boat with us from the start. Whereas we tried to get money for writing the script from Filmförder-ungsanstalt [German agency for film funding] and we got rejected with the reason that the film was not commercial enough.

SR: What are you working on now?

MvT: Going back to sisterhood. Making a film about sisters. The first one we did was *Marianne and Juliane* [1981].

BS: You made another sister film before, *Schwestern oder die Balance des Glücks* [1979].

MvT: And then there was *Fürchten und Lieben* [1988], filmed in Italy, which was an adaption of the *Three Sisters* by Anton Chekhov. And then I did *Die Schwester* [2009/10] and now comes the fifth sister film. This one has to do with my own history.

Film and History

Margarethe von Trotta / 2013

A lecture by Margarethe von Trotta, given at the University of Duisburg-Essen, Germany, December 10, 2013. Translated by Monika Raesch. Reprinted by permission of Margarethe von Trotta.

Margarethe von Trotta: First of all, I would like to thank you for the opportunity to speak to you today! For a film director, that's actually not an easy task, as our job normally entails listening and watching. Even before we start shooting, we have casting. Claude Chabrol, the French movie director, said to me: "My work is done when I have found the right actors for the roles; then they will do everything on their own." Of course, that exaggerates the role of casting, but good actors hold hands with the directors just as directors try to guide the actors down the path they [the directors] envision. Alfred Hitchcock, one of my masters besides Ingmar Bergman, at first always permitted actors to do whatever they envisioned—as his daughter shared. Only when he considered something to be entirely wrong, did he provide calm guidance to try it in "this or that way." He would provide this guidance with tact and discretion. And I share this approach. The influence the director has over the actor cannot be communicated in lectures or teaching; otherwise I would create an oppositional reaction. Since I was an actress myself before I was able to perform my dream job, directing movies, I am aware how actors can trick a director. If I had a specific vision of a scene that was unlike the one the director had, I first performed my version. I tried to provide the best performance possible. Then, I would perform the version he wanted me to execute as poorly as I possibly could, which resulted in him having to choose my version. Of course, he could not recognize my intention. Thus, I am forewarned and always on my toes to not be forced into visions that my cast prefers.

But acting and performance is not today's topic. As you perhaps know, many of my movies focus on history, especially German history of the past century. And with women. I am often asked why I always portray women [in my films]. Women

... well, I am a woman; one gets that point, though it often is met with incomprehension. Especially men always urge me to please focus on men for a change ... But history; why do I have such an interest in German history?

Possibly, I have to try to find a biographical explanation. I was born in Berlin, and my first memory of Germany, of Berlin, was post-WWII Berlin; [a city in] ruins. Meaning, I remember visuals of total destruction. When a child walks through Rome or Paris, holding mom's hand, the child subconsciously learns something about the history of the city and the country.

What could a child learn in postwar Berlin? Our mothers could not hold our hands and guide us into a life that we could glorify later. They were constantly worried that we would step on an [unexploded] mine since we could only play in the rubble and wreckage of houses; this happened occasionally. And they had to ensure that they could feed us, which often times took up all their time and energy. My mother, who had been born in Moscow and spoke Russian, would walk on foot from Schargendorf in the West through the entire city to the Russian sector to ask the commander for bread, which she did receive.

She belonged to a Baltic aristocratic family, which had lived in Moscow until the Russian Revolution. All Baltic residents were Russian nationals back then, as the Baltics belonged to the Czarist Empire. After the revolution, the family had to flee the now-communist country and, as a result, lost its citizenship. She—my mother—became, along with everybody else who had to flee, a stateless person, a person without national affiliation. Just like Hannah Arendt would at a later point in time, when she had to flee Nazi Germany.

To provide all stateless refugees with a new passport, the Norwegian arctic explorer and diplomat Friedthjof Nansen invented a new passport, called the Nansen-Pass. That permitted those people to at least have some form of identification, as without papers you were not only stateless but also vulnerable and unprotected. The issue has arisen again today; in France, you call people without citizenship "Les sans papiers"—those without papers.

In Germany, post World War II, the pass was called "alien passport." The cover was gray as opposed to green, which was the color of the cover of Germany's citizenship passport. Just the choice of the color symbolizes that one finds oneself in a "gray area." Since my mom was not married, I was also stateless and received the gray alien passport, even though I was born in Berlin. I only received the German passport as an adult, when I married a German citizen.

Being without national affiliation means that one is without a homeland; one is a foreigner in the country one was born in, attended school, and of which one speaks the language. And if one wanted to travel to any other country, one needed a visa and a recommendation letter. Unsurprisingly, I believe one of my favorite pieces of music is Schubert's "Winter Journey": "A stranger I arrived; a stranger I depart." I found an equivalent comment when Hannah Arendt said that she was "a girl from the outland."[1]

I moved as a "fille au pair" from Düsseldorf to Paris in the early sixties. Many girls and young women did this basically as a voluntary escape from musty Adenauer Germany.[2] Hanna Schygulla did the same. I not only discovered "free love" in France, I was also consciously confronted with German history for the first time. In 1950s Germany, in school, we learned about the Greeks and Romans, perhaps about Karl the Great, but definitely nothing about National Socialism. Not only our teachers, also our parents were silent on the subject. That's why I was interested in literature, art, and painting, not in history or politics. Regardless of how often I assured Parisian students that I was a "stateless" individual, they nonetheless viewed me as complicit in the killing of the Jews, in the German occupation of France, and so on.[3] I tried to defend myself, but I did not have the necessary knowledge to do so persuasively. I think this is a key reason I became interested in German history, not just about the history as historians present it, but the history that people lived, experienced, and witnessed.

It was the time of the building of the [Berlin] Wall, 1961. Suddenly, a wall ran through my birth city; people would be separated for years. Young French people could not understand my shock; for them, it was a fair punishment imposed on Germany. They were also too preoccupied with the Algerian War and the specific question how they could get out of military service. They had more empathy for the independence movement of the Algerians than with the suffering and despair of the victims of the German separation. That's when I started to open my eyes to the world.

When I began making movies later on—I directed my first film in 1977, *The Second Awakening of Christa Klages*—I had already been consuming our [German] history with great interest for a while. Prior to that, I had co-directed *The Lost Honor of Katharina Blum* with Volker Schlöndorff. That was an adaptation of a tale by Heinrich Böll. It's a story about 1970s Germany, in particular the angst-ridden society about terrorists and the *Bild* newspaper's hunting of allegedly left-wing followers. It's also a narrative about the origins of violence and what it can lead to.

It is my aim, using my own films and screening various film excerpts, to illustrate to you how my films differentiate themselves from general history and historical accounts. Even though my characters are embedded in German history, I never let a topic sway me, nor a specific historical time period [when making a movie]. I don't select a historical moment and then invent a plot for that. Instead, I select people and their fate—these are my inspirations that bind me to my film topics. I always ask myself whether the person I portray would actually choose to live in the specific time period if they had the choice of another time in which to live. Had I been able to select the moment of my birth, I certainly would not have chosen to be born in Berlin at the time of National Socialism. Let me provide you with an example from one of my films: I made a four-part TV series, *Jahrestage*,[4] based on Uwe Johnson's work. Character Gesine Cresspahl is born in Germany in 1933. And here comes my question: how does a person behave when they are born into a time period that asks them to be obedient and to accept a subordinate role? Does the person follow orders and become a subordinate, or does the person attempt to find a way to preserve one's own integrity and identity, even without becoming a hero? Does the person even have the possibility to think beyond the ideological constraints that the leaders impose? Hannah Arendt called this "thinking without a railing."[5] She felt that Eichmann was incapable of achieving that.

The same applies to terms, conditions, and sensitivities of a family or marriage. Those are also basically determined historically and upheld by laws. I also made movies about that.

Today, I only want to focus on that part of film history that occurred in one specific political time period that left Germany with deep marks. And I want to show you when a movie is permitted to take liberty with historical facts without distorting them.

I start with my film *Rosa Luxemburg*.

Rosa Luxemburg was born in the Galician part of Poland in 1870. To attend university, she moved to Switzerland. At that time, women were not yet permitted to study at German universities. She entered into a sham marriage, with a German in 1898, to earn German citizenship. She desired to work in the German social democratic movement. At the start of the century, it was the strongest political party in Europe; Rosa thought that her hopes of a revolution would be possible with that party. Instead of being satisfied with becoming a party member, to subordinate herself to August Bebel, Karl Kautsky, and comrades, she polemicizes and criticizes them to keep them motivated and not to settle for a comfortable bourgeois idyllic life; to not be satisfied by small successes. She wanted to remain a fighter working towards a revolution.

When the First World War arrives on the horizon in 1914, Rosa Luxemburg gives passionate speeches against the War and against Germany's participation. Her comrades, on the other hand, turn out to be nationalists; they vote for Germany's participation. Rosa Luxemburg is being put into custody to prevent her from continuing to work for an international unity and against the war. She remains detained in various prisons until the end of WWI.

Now, I want to show you the opening of my movie:

The first shot only shows sky and clouds above a dark wall. Then, a soldier appears, who walks on top of the wall. The camera tracks him. The soldier meets a second soldier, and turns around to continue his patrol. Only now that the camera slowly tracks down the wall; very slowly; the wall is very high, and far down below, in the ditch, we see Rosa Luxemburg walking as a prisoner in the snow. Only a raven accompanies her. Simultaneously, you hear her voice, replying to a letter by Sonja Liebknecht, Karl Liebknecht's wife. He—Karl Liebknecht—is also imprisoned, as he acted out against the war as well.

[1. Film excerpt]

What can you communicate with film visuals that can't be communicated verbally? Paolo Taviani, an Italian movie director, calls it: "writing with the camera."

Up high, in the sky,[6] symbol of freedom, the representatives of the reigning government are located. And Rosa, who dedicated herself for the freedom of all people, is relegated to the ground's depth. She is joined by a black bird, also a symbol for freedom; and it also stands for "knowledge" and "memory" in Germanic mythology. The snow's color signifies innocence and purity, while simultaneously being the color of a burial shroud. Shortly before her incarceration, Rosa had given a hopeful speech to workers: "Currently power still lies with those who support themselves solely with murder weapons; still wars are being prepared; still the God of War, Mars, is the man of the hour. But as Wallenstein said in Schiller's drama: the day is near; the day belongs to us. The day will near, on which we, those who stand down below, come to the top to realize a new order of society that is worthy of the human race; a society that doesn't know humans exploiting other humans; that doesn't know genocide; a society that realizes both the ideals of the oldest founders of religions as well as those of the biggest philosophers of mankind."[7]

At the end of Rosa's life, soldiers will still have power over her. The ditch in which they will throw her body will be turned into a trench for the Prussian and Imperial German Reserve Forces.[8] The movie opens at daytime; the movie ends at nighttime.

I will now show you a second excerpt from the same film. The scene plays on New Years Eve 1900 and features the German social democrats. August Bebel, the party's chairperson, gives a speech about hope and fulfillment, meaning the social democrat's expectations for the twentieth century.

At the time when I was writing the screenplay, only two witnesses of that time period were still alive.[9] Rosie Frölich was one. She had been Rosa's student, when Rosa had taught in the Party School. Rosi gifted me a picture that I had never seen before: Rosa dressed as a Geisha. I asked her what the purpose behind this masquerade was, and she explained that the social democrats would wear costumes at some of their festivities. Since Rosa was rather short—approximately 5 feet, 1.5 inches—and had dark hair, she had the idea of that particular costume. This photo provided me with an idea for my movie scene. I don't know whether the party [members] wore costumes at this New Years Eve party, but August Bebel's speech is authentic.

[2. Film excerpt]

As you saw: while Bebel speaks about his hopes for the new century, namely the realization of all hopes, he is surrounded by one giant bouquet of carnations situated behind and above him, with the white, innocent number 1900 in its center. Carnations were the party's flower. For the social democrats, red was the color of the revolution. For us, who now know what cruelty and shock the century brought, the color has turned into a humongous puddle of blood.

You can only see the color red in the movie four times. The first time, little Rosa waits patiently in front of a red rose bush, as she wants to see how a rose begins to bloom; later the grown-up Rosa similarly waits for the revolution to begin. When she finally gets released from prison, her female friend brings her a red rose as a greeting, mirroring Rosa's renewed hopes that finally the time of hopes becoming reality has arrived. Still, red foreshadows death.

Also in the excerpt that I want to show you next, red plays an important role. It is the end of the film.

Rosa Luxemburg and Karl Liebknecht are being brought to Berlin's Hotel Eden, and are then killed. After Rosa had been imprisoned in numerous prisons during the war, she assumes that she is being brought to yet another prison. She still believes in the history turning for the better, regardless of people. "We have the power in the state," she is mockingly told by Captain Waldemar Papst.[10] She answers, "History will prove the opposite."

A similar sentence is being said by another character of mine, Gudrun Ensslin, in the film *Marianne and Juliane* (1981). When she visits her sister in prison, she accuses her sister of not caring for her child but instead having focused on the world revolution. "You just wait, ten years . . . twenty. Only then will you be able to judge who of the two of us was right."

[3. Film excerpt]

As you saw, at the hotel, Rosa Luxemburg is being guided across a long red carpet. For me, this red carpet is a motif for the stream of blood that is still to be shed during this century. Rosa Luxemburg was a Jew, and she is being killed by "free regiments-soldiers"[11] that will later join Hitler's National Socialists. It's like you are in a fairytale by the Brothers Grimm, where all things have to happen three times to become true. "Twice more I will come, but never again. Once more I will come, but never again." You remember. First, Rosa is being hit on the head; that almost kills her. She is then shot (and killed) by an officer, who previously had assisted her putting on her coat. Finally, her body is being tossed into the canal. For sure, her murderers read Grimm's fairytales as children. And they are so afraid of this woman that they want to be certain that she can never return.

Now it is night (Hannah Arendt will speak about these dark times again later); the water is dark, contrasting the snow in the film's opening. I decided to keep the image on screen until the end of the closing credits. The water is deeper than a moat; and the water still flows there to this day. All the way to us. We can't detach ourselves from our history.

Sebastian Haffner wrote on the subject: "The murder on 15th January, 1919, was a beginning—the beginning of the thousands of murders occurring in the months that followed during the Noske-time period."[12] Followed by the millions of murders in the decades thereafter during the Hitler reign. That murder was the starting signal for all the others. And especially this one is still not admitted, is still unatoned, and without remorse. That's why he still screams into the German sky. That's why he still shines his searing light like a deathly laser beam into Germany's present time.

Often, I have been scolded by historians, at times in a rather mean manner, for not following historical facts to the letter. They call it "Geschichtsklitterung," [which would be translated as "glossing over history"]. In their eyes, a filmmaker does not have the right to add a dimension of the unsaid, of tragedy or poetry to historical facts.

In connection with this, I want to quote a Canadian historian, Bruno Ramirez. He is also the writer of my screenplay. "The power of film is also due to its language, a delicate mixture of the dramaturgical and visual, as opposed to the conceptual and explicatory written language of a historiographical text."

There is another reason why a film about history cannot be the same as a report a historian writes. We make movies to communicate with people who live in the present. My aim is to create a connection to the present when I work with historical material. For instance, Rosa Luxemburg fought on other fronts during her lifetime as well, not just the one against the war; she also fought against unions that didn't push for a revolution anymore, but instead had become sedate. She also fought against Eduard Bernstein, the man who asks her for a dance on New Years Eve in my movie. When I shot the film, in 1985, the peace movement was very strong in Germany. Big demonstrations occurred in Bonn against the exhibit of the Pershing rockets on German soil. Although Rosa agitated against the 1914 War in the movie, audiences connected it with the 1980s situation. And when I hosted a screening of the film in Israel, audiences applauded as they connected it to their wish for freedom and peace.

I want to briefly speak about another person who knew people from Rosa's time, who I was able to question as part of my research. He helped me to discover aspects of Rosa that went beyond any classic description. I already told you about Rosie Frölich.

It was the old anarchist Alexander Souchy. He was already way beyond ninety years old when I met him, and had lived a rather exciting life. He lived the typical life of a resilient left-wing supporter in Europe. In Russia, he had met Pjotr Fjodorowitch Kropotkin, the prince/ruler of the Anarchists; during the Spanish Civil War he fought against Franco; lived for a long time in Cuba, and lived in Munich when I met him shortly before his death. He had held on to a beautiful sense of humor and shared a story about Rosa's cat with me in a rather amusing way. Rosa had trained her cat, Mimi, so that she was able to also sit at the table like a person and to eat civilized out of her bowl.

I will show you this scene excerpt.

[4. Film excerpt]

Of course, you won't be able to find this scene in any history book. But I was able to communicate [to the cinema audience] Rosa's loneliness, her isolation, just by having such a scene, without words or speeches; no talking was necessary. It represents the peace and quiet following the turmoil.

The next movie I directed that dealt with German history is *Rosenstrasse* (2003). This movie also is centered on women who don't want to accept the fate that the government has bestowed upon them. The movie is set during World War II, in Berlin, February 1943. During the so called "Fabrikaktion"—roughly translated as "factory action"—Jewish men who at that time lived in a mixed marriage, meaning they were married to non-Jewish German women and were thus "safe," were moved into a house in the Rosenstrasse [name of a particular street]. The house was located near the Hackeschen Höfen.[13] They were scheduled to be transported to Auschwitz from there; back then it was called "evacuation." That's at least what the women expected and feared. They gather in front of the house and don't leave at all. As more women join every day, Josef Goebbels, the Propaganda Minister and Gauleiter,[14] becomes concerned—the foreign press had already heard about this situation—and releases the men. He jots down in his diary that he will recapture every single one of these men once the commotion has died down.

I want to show you an excerpt in which the Nazis attempt to scare the women so that they leave the street.

[5. Film excerpt]

Why couldn't they simply shoot the women, given that they felt no inhibitions to kill others? The reason apparently was the following: these were not Jewish women, and thus embodied the ideal of loyalty, a virtue that was supported by the Nazis. The soldiers fighting at the front had to trust that their wives and fiancées would be faithful to them. If you ask me, that's the reason why these women from the former GDR[15] were honored so late. The Rosenstrasse was located in East Berlin. If they would have pushed for their men's release for pure political reasons, they would have most likely been added to the Pantheon as heroes of the resistance. But given the circumstances, they were simply "only" women who stayed by their husbands' side out of love. And there's no space for love in historical chronicles.

Several leftist historians already were ruffled in regards to *Rosa Luxemburg*, since I took the lives of the wives and women as serious as those of the politicians and revolutionaries. Marxist teachings favor dispositions, and it was very difficult for me to even locate a biography about Rosa Luxemburg that included something about her role as a woman. Lucky for me, she left behind 2,500 letters; and letters are the best sources to come close to a person so that one can connect the political and the personal, and to even explain the former with the latter. "The private is the political"—that was a slogan of the 1970s feminist movement. Rosa Luxemburg complained often that her comrades would speak differently in private versus public settings. Given that she demanded better of others, she had to follow the same ideals [saying the same thing privately and publicly]. I think that that's still a relevant topic today.

In reality, if I can trust the people who lived during Rosa's time period and lived in the Rosenstrasse, many more women were standing in the street than you just saw [in my movie excerpt]. In the end, apparently more than a thousand women and children persevered and protested. The movie production could not or did not want to permit me that many extras; so in the end I had a maximum of three hundred [women and children in the street]. From a historian's perspective, that's the wrong number. What was important for me, however, was to show that at the start only a few women protested. But with every new day, the numbers grew, meaning that more and more women found the courage to disobey the Nazi rules. Maybe one should say "civil courage"? In *Hannah Arendt*, a judge asks Eichmann: "If more people had had civil courage, would things have turned out differently?" And Eichmann replies: "Yes, if civil courage would have a hierarchy." In my viewpoint, he confirms Hannah Arendt's suspicion that Eichmann—while he was not stupid—was thoughtless.

Here's another example. I am pretty sure you all know the movie *Amadeus* (1984) by Milos Forman, about the life of Mozart. Mozart became increasingly poorer throughout his lifetime; he had to move ten times, and he eventually died in complete poverty. It would be preposterous to show him moving home ten times. As a result, Foreman solved this dilemma by slowly but surely having the decorations in Mozart's first apartment become poorer and look miserable. This resulted in the same effect.

There is a moment in *Rosenstrasse* where I imagined a scene that did not exist; it could have happened, but I could not find any proof of it. Fact is that you still had movie premieres at the beginning of 1943. Possibly, Goebbels participated in those in his role as film and propaganda minister. However, Goebbels was also NSDAP Gauleiter[16] in Berlin, meaning his jurisdiction included the Rosenstrasse. He was also known to be a womanizer; his nickname was "the buck from Babelsberg."[17] The scene illustrates that at that moment in time, life in Germany still included carefree parties and the attempt to "forget" about the upcoming defeat. In fact, these people were so focused on their enjoyment that they did not realize that the movie star—she is loosely based on Lizzie Waldmüller—sings an inappropriate[18] song, composed by a Jewish artist. The lyrics specifically contradict everything that the National Socialists ask from women, in particular loyalty.

[6. Film excerpt]

A well-known German historian accused me of altering historical facts, as I suggest that Goebbels released the men because he had sex with one of the women; the woman being played by Katja Riemann. That, in fact, would have been a serious twist on the truth. But if you watched the movie closely, you notice that Katja Riemann cries as her actions and those of her brother have not made any difference; and that the idea of sleeping with Goebbels was an idea that rose out of complete desperation. Her rather naïve plan was: let her beauty attract Goebbels so that her brother can edge closer and persuade him to set the men free. The moment in which her brother opens her buttons of her borrowed dress proves this. A minister who is known as a "wild buck"[19] would not have stopped from appreciatively and completely unbuttoning Katja's dress. Those are the hints and clues filmmakers provide that are often overlooked by historians; however, they are important to fully understand the narrative and its context. "Writing with the camera."

The men have been released. Supposedly, some documents prove that the "prisoners"[20] of the Rosenstrasse were not scheduled to be brought to a concentration camp. The people who lived during the time period and who I could speak with, however, were all convinced that only the women's actions, their perseverance, resulted in the victory of their men having been released. As I said already in the beginning, I base my films on the subjective lives of people. I connected myself to their accounts. Even if this should not completely and accurately represent historical truth, it does not diminish the courageous actions by these women.

Returning to Rosa Luxemburg; she is an idealist and utopist who believed in history and progress; she viewed these as a wiser viewpoint than the viewpoints of people. In 1905, she wrote: "History of society exhibits feverish labor pains;

social compositions push to the surface. New is to come."[21] And in 1917, she wrote from prison: "History always knows best; knows where it hopelessly got lost in a dead-end street."[22] And in 1918: "History alone knows best for its own worries, and it already exploded some dunghills that stood in its way. It will persevere this time as well."[23]

The women from the Rosenstrasse no longer believe in a utopia, don't believe in a future; they live in a scary presence, during the "dark days" as Hannah Arendt labeled this time period. The women no longer have the dream to save all human kind, but only have the desperate wish to save their men.

In the last movie that I want to introduce you to today, Hannah Arendt reflects back to the terror that was totalitarianism. She was also a Jew, but she was smart enough to predict the developments in Germany under Hitler and flee Germany in a timely manner. Nonetheless, perhaps Hannah Arendt continued to believe in a utopia; not Rosa Luxemburg who trusted in history; Arendt's utopia was that of a philosopher who trusted in the process of thinking. Perhaps she expected to receive the strength that Rosa gathered from her belief in history. Bettina Stangneth, a contemporary German philosopher and Arendt specialist explained that Arendt found the thought that an evil philosophy could emerge unbearable.

The scene I am about to show most likely did not take place in the way it is depicted. I found the text that Hannah Arendt presents in one of her letters addressed to Karl Jaspers, who was her dissertation chair and friend. Whether she ever taught a "German course" in the United States is unknown to me. But I needed the text in which she speaks about people making other people redundant, especially since she still believes in the "radical evil" at that time. Only once she has to describe Adolf Eichmann and realizes that the term "radical evil" cannot be applied to him does she evolve the concept into that of "banality of evil."

[7. Film excerpt]

If you have watched the movie, you will remember that I did not cast an actor in the role of Eichmann but instead cut black and white documentary-like archival footage into my film. My aim was to permit the viewer to share with Hannah Arendt's observations, doubts, and insights. However, how can we pretend that the actress literally sits across from the real Eichmann? Stylistically, it would have been impossible to use the courtroom that still exists in Jerusalem. Since the pressroom, located directly underneath the courtroom, fed American television reports on several monitors, I decided to position Hannah Arendt into the pressroom. I even justified this decision to myself, by focusing on her smoking addiction. Smoking was not permitted in the courtroom. Sometimes you think you invent something since it helps you stylistically; but looking back, you realize that you really only helped to surface the truth.

A nephew [of Arendt's] who saw the movie during its first screening in Israel said to me afterwards: "Hannah smoked much more than she did in your film. That's why she followed the court proceedings almost entirely from the pressroom."

And now one last excerpt from the end of the film. Hannah Arendt just concluded her closing speech to the student body. It included her hopes that thinking will save people from catastrophes. Her friend from teenage years, Hans Jonas, listened to the speech as well and accused her heavily. This encounter also did not take place the way it was depicted in the film. Following the publication of Hannah Arendt's article in the *New Yorker*, Hans Jonas wrote her a letter ending their friendship. Hans Jonas's widow, who I was fortunate enough to still meet in person, kindly gave me the letter. This letter has never been published.

[8. Film excerpt]

My film *Hannah Arendt* also was not viewed positively by historians. They accused me of incompetence as I omitted the most recent insights into Eichmann. According to them, I was noncritical of Hannah Arendt, and thus I honored her by simply supporting her viewpoints and arguments. They are not completely wrong saying that. I adore Hannah Arendt, I admire her independent thinking. I attempted to follow one of her guiding principles: I WANT TO UNDERSTAND. I tried to understand what she saw in Adolf Eichmann; why she saw him as a mediocre, incompetent-to-think bureaucrat. That's another reason why I added the archival footage. But that doesn't mean that I wanted to make a documentary or did make one. My film remains a piece of fiction; it attempts to make correspondences that are only possible to understand via the visuals.

I will show you this one last time by looking at the opening of *Hannah Arendt*. You will see. At the beginning, the screen is black. It's night, just as it is at the end of *Rosa Luxemburg*. Then, you see two lights coming towards us out of the distance and darkness. They look like eyes that look at us from the depth of the darkness, before they become identifiable as the lights of buses. Hannah Arendt often spoke about the "gloomy days." For me, the film's opening means: it will speak to us from the past about the dark times. Then you see Hannah Arendt lighting a cigarette; it appears as though she is already connected spiritually with Eichmann. Pondering, she slowly walks through her dark apartment and lies down on the couch. [That's] her "thought posture," as Mary McCarthy described it. This spiritual connection with Eichmann will be the story of the film. Although he won't be shown as a person, he accompanies her until she is able to describe and understand him. Even further, he accompanies her into controversy. At the end of the film, Hannah is again located in her thought posture on the couch. Thinking about evil will remain with her until her death.

[9. Film excerpt]

History and film. Facts and fantasy. How far can a filmmaker remove him/
herself from the pure historical facts? Of course, there would have been better
examples than my own movies. But I wanted to use this approach to also tell you
something about myself.

And one last time *Hannah Arendt*. There's a moment in the film when the *New
Yorker's* editor asks her whether her description of the Jewish councils was perhaps an interpretation. Hannah Arendt replied sharply: "It's a fact." In her closing remarks, however, she acknowledges that her description originated from a
philosophical viewpoint.

I thank you.

Notes

1. The word "outland" was chosen over "foreign land" as it is used more often in a poetic
context.

2. Konrad Adenauer was the chancellor of Germany from 1949 to 1963.

3. Von Trotta used the German idiom "boche" to describe such a person.

4. *Jahrestage* (2000) has not received distribution in an English-speaking country and no
English title exists. Closely translated, the title would be "Anniversaries."

5. The above is a literal translation of Arendt's words, "Denken ohne Geländer." The German
book under the same title is not available in English. Elsewhere in this volume, the word has
also been translated as "banister."

6. Arguably, this word could also be translated as "heaven"; the German language uses
the same word for both "sky" and "heaven." It is unclear from the context which meaning
von Trotta intended in her speech. She may have also chosen to have audiences decide the
meaning for themselves.

7. Rosa's speeches are published in book form and online. While the editor of this volume
noticed discrepancies between the excerpt von Trotta used and official print versions of
Rosa's speech, she kept von Trotta's version and translated it to stay faithful to von Trotta's
presentation.

The German text von Trotta quoted and that is translated into English above is the
following:

Noch liegt die Macht bei denjenigen, die sich allein auf eine Welt voll Mordwaffen
stützen, noch werden Kriege vorbereitet, noch regiert der Kriegsgott Mars die Stunde.
Aber wie Wallenstein im Schiller'schen Drama sagte: Der Tag ist nah, der Tag der uns
gehört. So wird der Tag nahen, an dem wir, die unten stehen, nach oben kommen
werden, um eine Gesellschaftsordnung wahr zu machen, die des Menschengeschlechts
würdig ist, eine Gesellschaft, die keine Ausbeutung des Menschen durch den

Menschen kennt, die keinen Völkermord kennt, eine Gesellschaft, die die Ideale
sowohl der ältesten Religionsstifter als auch der grössten Philosophen der Menschheit
verwirklichen wird.

8. The German word used by von Trotta to describe these trenches is "Landwehrkanal," with
"Landwehr" being the term used to describe the Prussian and Imperial German Forces.

9. Von Trotta's wording leaves it somewhat unclear whether only two witnesses of the time
period were still alive or whether she could only speak to two of multiple witnesses.

10. Waldemar Papst's complete German title was Generalstabs-Offizier der Garde-
Kavallerie-Schützen-Division, and von Trotta uses his entire title in her speech. (His title is not
translated in several English biographies.)

11. Free regiment or Freikorps soldiers, known in German as Freikorps-Soldaten, were
German volunteer units that existed from the eigthteenth to early twentieth century. They
fought as mercenaries regardless of their nationality. (Source: Wikipedia)

12. This is a reference to Gustav Noske, minister of defense of the Weimar Republic between
1919 and 1920. He used armed forces to suppress uprisings in 1919. (Source: Wikipedia)

13. They are a specific art nouveau courtyard complex in Berlin's center, designed in 1906.

14. This second position has not been translated into English; Goebbels is generally only
labeled as a "minister."

15. GDR stands for the German Democratic Republic, also known as the former East
Germany, which existed from 1949 until 1990. (West and East) Germany reunited on October 3,
1990.

16. NSDAP is the abbreviation for the Nationalsozialistische Deutsche Arbeiterpartei/The
National Socialist German Workers' Party, commonly referred to as the Nazi Party.

17. Von Trotta stated that the German nickname was "Bock von Babelsberg." "Buck" is
a German idiom for a womanizer, and "Babelsberg" refers to the specific location in which
Goebbels was known to be a womanizer.

18. Von Trotta uses the word "frivol" for which there is no direct English translation. The
inappropriateness of the song is illuminated via the description in the sentence thereafter.

19. Von Trotta calls him a "geilen Bock."

20. Von Trotta opted to not use the term "prisoner" but the word "Einsitzender," which
does not have a direct English translation. Her word choice would leave it open whether the
men were held against their will. For instance, protesters who don't leave a room in which they
protest can also be referred to as "Einsitzende."

21. Her words were: "Die Geschichte der Menschheit fiebert in Geburtswehen, neue soziale
Gestaltungen drängen ans Licht. Es wird Neues warden."

22. Her words were: "Die Geschichte weiss stets am besten Rat, wo sie sich am
hoffnungslosesten in die Sackgasse verlaufen zu haben scheint."

23. Her words were: "Die Geschichte allein weiss Rat für ihre eigenen Sorgen, und sie hat
schon manchen Misthaufen in die Luft gesprengt, der ihr im Weg stand. Sie wird's auch diesmal
schaffen."

Approaching a Biography: Rosa Luxemburg, Hildegard von Bingen, Hannah Arendt

Margarethe von Trotta / 2014

A lecture by Margarethe von Trotta, given at the University of Duisburg-Essen, Germany, February 11, 2014. Reprinted by permission of Margarethe von Trotta.

After my film *Hannah Arendt* came out, Piper Verlag, Munich, which published almost all of Hannah Arendt's writings, suggested I write a book about Arendt. Initially, I was surprised by the proposal, since, as I saw it, there are already so many books, biographies, and texts about her that there wasn't really any need for me to add yet another one. But then they explained to me that it wasn't a new biography that they had in mind, but rather that they wanted me to describe my approach to Arendt and how I "unlearned being afraid of her."

I turned down the offer because I wanted to let my film speak for itself and couldn't imagine that readers might be interested in my doubts or fears. The editor was disappointed by my refusal. Unlike me, she was convinced that people who had enjoyed the film might be curious to find out why I had taken on such a significant woman and philosopher and whether I hadn't sometimes lost my nerve.

Today, in front of this audience, I will try belatedly to comply with this request. And I'll describe the challenges of this approach using not just my film about Hannah Arendt, but also those about two other historical female figures: Hildegard von Bingen and Rosa Luxemburg.

In doing so, I'd like to quote a statement Hannah Arendt made in an interview late in her life: "I would like to say that everything I did and everything I wrote—all that is tentative. I think that all thinking . . . has the earmark of being tentative."

The same is true of anything I may say in and about any of my films.

What does it mean for a filmmaker to expose herself to a historical figure? Because, if you don't expose yourself, if you don't attempt to recognize, to see yourself reflected in him or her, to struggle to achieve an intimacy of sorts with someone who started off as a stranger to you, ultimately your viewers won't be able to sympathize with this person either.

As I've already pointed out, Hannah Arendt isn't the only woman in my film-making life I've tried to win over, as it were. That said, I suspected from the start that she would make it even harder for me than the others. Unlike her American writer friend Mary McCarthy, Arendt was extremely reticent about discussing her private life and feelings, especially with strangers. Yet merely exploring a person at the intellectual level isn't enough for me.

There are films that emerge entirely from within you. You sit down and begin to let your imagination roam and it's as if you were opening a zipper to your unconscious and, with it, of course, to your own hidden life. That's what happened to me with my film *Sisters, or The Balance of Happiness*. In it, I presaged or intuited that I have a sister, whom I'd known nothing about until that point.

And then there are films, material, or figures that are brought to you from the outside, which you initially refuse to believe you might have anything in common with and for which it takes you a long time to develop a feel for the "correspondences," in Baudelaire's sense of the term.

It wasn't my idea to make a movie about Hannah Arendt. Martin Wiebel, an old friend, longtime supporter of my films, and an editor at WDR, downright ambushed me with the idea after I had finished shooting *Rosenstrasse*. It had been an extremely strenuous shoot and I had been planning to take my time to think about my next film project. So my immediate reaction was to shake my head; his suggestion made no sense to me: A movie about a philosopher whose principal pursuits were thinking and writing? Completely impossible; you can't represent that on film. And, with that, for the time being, the subject was off the table for me.

But after a while I remembered that I'd had a similar knee-jerk reaction before. Rainer Werner Fassbinder's last project had been a film about Rosa Luxemburg, and after his death his producer had approached me, declaring that I owed it to my friendship with Fassbinder to take over the film. Especially since I was a woman. This—in the fall of 1982—was the first time I was hearing that my being a woman might work to my advantage! I turned down the offer.

At the time, I didn't know that much about Rosa Luxemburg, even though she was one of the icons of the Sixty-Eight generation, her picture showing up alongside portraits of Marx, Lenin, and Ho Chi Minh on the signs students carried through the streets back then. Just this one lone woman in the midst of all these men. I had noticed that she looked rather sad and not as defiant as you'd expect for a revolutionary. This contradiction had sparked my curiosity. Maybe this was a reason to give in to the producer's urging after all. Contradictions have always appealed to me. I did set one condition, though: namely, that I would be allowed to write my own screenplay; in other words, that I could find out what about Rosa Luxemburg resonated with me—with me personally. In the mood for love, as it were.

I often deal with history in my films and, in doing so, try to draw a connection to my own biography. Rosa Luxemburg was a revolutionary; my mother and her family, as Baltic aristocrats, were expelled from Moscow by the very revolution Rosa enthusiastically supported, and they become stateless and homeless as a result. As a child, all I ever heard was that their misfortune was the Bolsheviks' fault, and some of them had even been grateful to Hitler for starting the war against Russia.

My mother read the memoirs of Alexander Fyodorovich Kerensky, Wolfgang Leonhard's *Child of the Revolution*, and other writers who had broken with communism. She read neither Marx nor Rosa Luxemburg. Suddenly I saw the offer to make a movie about Luxemburg—and consequently about a period I hadn't experienced myself—as an opportunity to understand something about our past: Where did we come from and what had this century done with us?

It was a long, you could almost say rocky road—that is, a road across a great deal of asphalt. In order to consult unpublished texts by Rosa Luxemburg, I had to trek to the Institute of Marxism-Leninism in East Berlin. Every time I went there, I had to take the S-Bahn to the Friedrichstrasse station. The platforms were patrolled by Vopos—East Germany's People's Police; at the passport control counter, I would be rudely ordered to show my ear, and I never once managed to elicit so much as a hint of a smile from the impassive controllers. From the Friedrichstrasse station, to reach the institute, I had to cross Karl-Liebknecht Strasse and walk to the corner of Pieck-Allee. It was only thanks to a misunderstanding that I had even been allowed to enter this temple of Marxism.

At the time, access was denied to many West German historians and scholars. The reason I had escaped this ban was that, completely ingenuously, I had joined a West German peace movement that, as I later discovered, was financed by East Germany.

As a result, the censors assumed that I was favorably disposed to East Germany, maybe even a member of the German Communist Party. Even so, I wasn't allowed to take a single unsupervised step; even when I went to the smoking room—I was still a smoker at the time—a historian would accompany me, always having to pretend that he was dying for a cigarette, too.

Luckily, I soon met the institute's Rosa Luxemburg expert, Annelies Laschitza, whom I'm friends with to this day. But even she, despite our friendship, was required to report back about me—as I learned from the Gauck papers after the fall of the Wall. She did so without denouncing me. She even warned me, despite being a member of the party, not to pursue a co-production with East Germany. "They'll expect you to make a cinematic hagiography, just like our film about Clara Zetkin," she cautioned me. I took her warning to heart.

For me, this research—like my research for my film *Rosenstrasse* later on— ended up being like a belated history lesson.

I not only spent many weeks traveling to East Berlin, but to Warsaw as well, where Rosa Luxemburg spent time in prison at the beginning of the century. Yet the more I learned of and about Rosa Luxemburg, the more insecure I became. A Polish colleague of mine, a vehement anti-communist like so many Poles at the time, told me: "Leave her in the Landwehr Canal where she belongs; why are you trying to pull her back out?"

In the biographies, mostly written by leftist historians, I found virtually nothing about her private life. They were about the Party, the correct interpretation of Marxism, and the class struggle, but not about love or friendships—especially not those that weren't strictly political in nature. And, reading these biographies, I felt a little like Rosa Luxemburg herself, who once complained in a letter to Leo Jogiches, her Polish lover and comrade: "Pages and pages of information about the work of the Party, but not a crumb of normal life. I was so tired sometimes that I almost passed out from your scribbling. When did we actually truly live?" Normal life—where could I find out something about it? Fortunately, Rosa left behind some 2,500 letters. They provided me with information about her likes and dislikes, her amorous encounters and her moments of despair.

And yet! To get to the hidden parts of her character, I even resorted to the Active Imagination technique described by C. G. Jung. You sit down on the floor, close your eyes, and wait for what your imagination offers up. I decided to meet Rosa in this way, so that she could reveal things to me that I couldn't find in the books. During one of these sessions—just to give you an example of how this works—she told me: "Remember that I had very beautiful long hair, and whenever I was with a man I would spread it out over him." There are, after all, only photographs of her in which she wears her hair pinned up, like all women did at the time, so we automatically make the mistake of only imaging this chaste version of her.

My search for her—not least using this adventurous approach—took me on a veritable emotional roller-coaster ride. Reading one of her letters to a friend, she struck me as warmhearted and likable; reading a speech against the members of the Party, she seemed self-righteous and arrogant. Then I'd go back to reading her letters, and would find myself admiring her again. Occasionally she'd get on my nerves with her infatuation with plants and birds, and I'd have to pick up one of her incisive political texts again. That's how it went for a while, back and forth, until she became increasingly clear and three-dimensional to me as a person, and increasingly rich and contradictory, too.

As my idea of her became increasingly solid and nuanced, I was once again gripped by fear. How could I convey this complexity, the richness of her personality, in a two-hour film?

Ultimately, my admiration carried the day. How she challenged and goaded the men of the social democracy again and again; how she laid siege—in word and deed—to this phalanx of indolence. And I was moved by her confidence. As a member of the postwar generation, who already knew the horrors the twentieth century held in store, I was touched by her belief that everything would take a turn for the better despite the adverse times. Even from within prison, she encouraged her friends, advising them to have faith in history, so much wiser than humanity.

Two years into my research, I began to trust her and my idea of her. I recognized many aspects of my own life in hers. *Toute proportion gardée*, of course. I, too, often had to defend myself against male prejudices and scorn. For Rosa, there was the added fact that she was Jewish, and many in the society at the time, even in her party, were anti-Semitic. There are caricatures of her that would cause an outcry today. And how often she was dismissed as a "hysterical woman," even by her own comrades. This allegation of hysteria, usually lobbed at smart women trying to assert themselves and their ideas, is still familiar to us today.

Rosa Luxemburg, however, was no feminist. No more so than Hannah Arendt was. Both were exceptions and, as such, felt no need to take a stand for other women. Seen from the point of view of the present, however, they conform to everything that feminists desire for and from women. And yet, ultimately it was something else that drew me to them: both women—who appeared to be so exceptionally strong seen from the outside—were no strangers to loneliness, sadness, romantic betrayal, and pain. It's these hidden aspects of them—their second face, you could say—that allowed me to feel close to them.

In conclusion, I will read to you from one of Rosa Luxemburg's letters that conveys her capacity for suffering and compassion.

She wrote it while in prison to Sonja Liebknecht, the wife of Karl Liebknecht, her comrade-in-arms:

Oh, Sonitschka, I experienced a sharp pain here. A few days ago, a wagon loaded with sacks drove into the prison. The cargo was piled so high that the oxen couldn't make it over the threshold of the gateway. The soldier accompanying them, a brutal character, began to beat the animals so savagely that one of them bled. . . . Then, during the unloading, the animals just stood there, completely still, exhausted, the one that was bleeding staring ahead with an expression on its black face like that of a tear-stained child. I stood before it and the animal looked at me, tears streaming down my face— they were its tears; you couldn't wince with greater pain for your dearest brother than I did in my powerlessness over this silent suffering. Oh, my poor buffalo, my poor, beloved brother, we both stand here so silently, united only in pain, powerlessness and longing . . . Sonitschka, dearest, in spite of it all, be calm and cheerful. That's life and that's how one must take it: courageously, intrepidly and smilingly—in spite of all.

The first time I read this letter, I knew I had to include it in my film. It allowed me to contradict the image of bloody red Rosa that many people still predominantly had of her at the time. In the 1970s, there was a postage stamp with a portrait of Luxemburg on it. And there were actually people who refused to accept a letter if it had this stamp on it.

I've already mentioned the importance of letters in helping me approach a historical figure. The same is true of Hildegard von Bingen. Approaching her was, on the one hand, more difficult because the era in which she lived seems so infinitely far from us—an era in which people still believed that the world was flat; on the other, for that same reason, I also felt freer towards her. When we think about the beginning of the last century, we still feel a certain connection—there are photographs of the period and even moving images. But the Middle Ages?

Hildegard was born in 1098 and died in 1179, reaching the age—very unusual for the time—of eighty-one years. Nun, visionary, abbess, healer, researcher, composer, believer. I am neither a nun, nor a scientist or composer, and I grew up Protestant. So what could possibly lead me to her? Nothing but my curiosity and many questions. The most important of which for me was: What did this distant era have to offer—in today's sense of the word—an intelligent and talented woman? Did she have the opportunity to recognize her gifts? And how was she able to assert them?

The women of the early years of the so-called new women's movement in the 1970s—the Nazis had also amputated and rendered grotesque the women's movement—were looking for role models from the past. Did they even exist? After all, women almost only appeared in history books if they were rulers like Queen Elizabeth of England or Catherine the Great of Russia. Apart from them, world history was made and described by men. And while these men may have had mothers, wet nurses, governesses, cooks, lovers, or wives, . . . apparently, they didn't have much to say about them—unless they possessed a certain political power as lovers, like Madame de Pompadour.

I begin the film by showing a group of people at the end of the first millennium. Many people then believed that the world would end during the night to the year 1000 and they prepared for it with self-chastisement and prayer. Not unlike how we feared the year 2000, because we thought the computer world would collapse. I imagined how inconceivable it must have seemed to people back then when the sun came up again the next morning, the world still existed and they were still alive. The sun. Light. The night was over; a new era was dawning. And it was in the first century of this new era that Hildegard was born and received messages from the "living light."

In the very beginning of the film I let the young Hildegard ride gradually from blurriness and indistinctness into visibility. To me, that means: she is approaching us from the distant past. And we will watch her through the eyes of our present-day secular knowledge.

My first trip this time was to the Hildegard convent in Eibingen near Rüdesheim. There, I met Sister Philippa, who, as a former journalist, is responsible for contact with the outside world. She eagerly provided me with information, like Annelies Laschitza had for Rosa Luxemburg. She advised me on which biography I should read—Barbara Beuys's *Denn ich bin krank vor Liebe* (*For I Am Sick with Love*); unfortunately, an infinite amount of trash and kitsch has been written about Hildegard—and pointed me to her correspondence in particular. Sister Philippa asked just one thing of me: "Please, not too many herbs. Don't turn her into an herb lady." As you may know, Hildegard is known today primarily for her herbal knowledge; there are pharmacies named after her, mueslis and teas and all kinds of alternative medicine treatments. But I really wasn't interested in reducing her to her herbal knowledge.

At the end of our first meeting, Sister Philippa invited me to a profession—that is, someone taking her final vows—at the convent two weeks later. A real opportunity for me, since hardly any young women want to become nuns anymore. I was then able to speak with this nun, as well as with her father, who had come to the novices' reception celebration—a craftsman, who didn't hide his displeasure at his daughter's decision from me.

I was very impressed by the young woman and her delight—so seemingly genuine—at being allowed to take the veil. In the Middle Ages, joining a convent wasn't uncommon. Hildegard was given over to the Church already as a little girl, as payment for the so-called "tenth" (the tenth child), with no opportunity to object. She did not join the convent voluntarily.

How does a person act who is born into an era she didn't choose, into a society that wants to force her to behave in certain ways? Will she try to think "without a banister," as Hannah Arendt put it? Hildegard's banisters were Christianity, the Bible, the psalms, the Word of God. How did she manage to recognize her strengths and desires within the confines of these clearly defined borders? And how did she manage to express them?

Hildegard had visions and was convinced that they were sent to her by God. But at first she wasn't sure if she could even talk about them. After all, she could have been accused of receiving these visions from the devil. Which would have meant excommunication—a death sentence of sorts for a person of faith, eternal damnation.

Today, we know that particularly severe migraines can trigger hallucinations like these—Oliver Sacks has written very impressively about it. We can assume that this was the case of Hildegard's visions, since she suffered from poor health her entire life and repeatedly had to retire to her bed for weeks at a time.

After writing down her visions, she turned in all humility to Bernhard von Clervaux, the most powerful clergyman of his time, to ask him to take it to the Pope for his authentication. This was, to put it a bit flippantly, her first coup: Hildegard managed to get the Church to recognize her as a visionary. And, with that, she no longer owed obedience to her abbot. Next, the voice ordered her to found her own convent and to leave behind the one where she was supposed to stay until her death.

From a mixed monastery, where both monks and nuns reside, Hildegard now switched to a convent for women only, where, in keeping with the rules of the Benedictines, she was the sole authority. What fascinated me about Hildegard was how this smart woman succeeded in emancipating herself, as we would put it today, from the rules of her time even as she continued to believe firmly that she was obeying God's voice and God's voice alone. She couldn't see that it was actually the voice of her own unconscious and secret desires. As a result, she continued to believe that women were weak. She repeatedly emphasized: "I am but a weak woman." Even so, she didn't escape the wrath of the men of her time. Many revered her, but many would have welcomed her excommunication. The fact that it took almost a thousand years before she was canonized by a pope supports this hypothesis.

So, with Hildegard von Bingen it was once again the contradictions in her biography that appealed to me. On the one hand, as an abbess and visionary, she corresponded with the powerful men of her time, with emperors and popes, even admonishing them and giving them orders—since these orders weren't coming from her but from God. On the other hand, when a young nun, Richardis von Stade, whom she had grown particularly close to, wanted to go her own way to become an abbess in her own right at another convent, Hildegard turned into a completely ordinary, loving woman driven to frenzied behavior by passion and pain.

To try to get Richardis back to her convent and back to her, Hildegard even wrote to the Pope, but he rebuffed her. In the end, she had to resign herself to her fate.

Here is an excerpt from a letter she wrote to Richardis von Stade:

Woe is me, mother, woe is me, daughter. Why have you left me behind like an orphan? I loved the nobility of your manners, your wisdom and chasteness, your soul and your whole life, to the point that many said: "What are you doing?" Now everyone suffering a pain like my pain must lament with me, anyone who has felt love for a person out of the love of God in their hearts and soul, as I did for you—a person wrested from them in an instant, as you were wrested from me.

May the angel of God walk before you, may the Son of God protect you and may his mother watch over you. Remember your poor mother Hildegard, so that your good fortune doesn't fade away.

"So that your good fortune doesn't fade away . . . !" That sounds a bit like a veiled threat, doesn't it? Which can also be understood as a vision, since, as it happens, Richardis died just a year after leaving Hildegard's convent. And it is difficult not to suspect that Hildegard, in some small corner of her heart, wished for her death, just as women today sometimes do when abandoned by their lovers.

And now on to Hannah Arendt!

When, after my initial resistance, I decided to at least try to approach her life and work, I began by listening to her famous conversation with Günter Gaus, a German TV-anchor, at first just as an audio recording. She struck me as arrogant and self-righteous, constantly interrupting and correcting Gaus. To the point that I immediately considered abandoning the project, before I had even really started it. Not long afterwards, I watched the same conversation on DVD and was surprised by what a different impression she made on me. Charming and captivating. And I could understand Gaus, who, when asked once who his favorite conversation partner was, had answered: Hannah Arendt. He and his wife had been truly in love in with her. I, on the other hand, was far from being in love.

Günter Gaus told another story that may also come as a surprise to us: Hannah Arendt, he said, was so nervous before the conversation started, and even during the recording, that he was worried she might get up and leave the studio. Thankfully, one of the cameramen—in 1963, cameras were still enormous machines, very difficult to move—interrupted suddenly, saying that he couldn't keep shooting like this—there was a nail sticking out of the floor that the camera kept getting stuck on; he couldn't work this way. And so Gaus and Hannah went back to the dressing room, smoked a few cigarettes, chatted, and came back to the set once the problem with the nail had been resolved. And from that point on, Hannah was calm, any noticeable nervousness gone. So, as it turns out, we have a nail to thank for this marvelous document.

Later, in New York, Hannah Arendt's last assistant, Jerome Kohn, confirmed to me that Hannah suffered from serious stage fright before every lecture and speech she had to give. I had thought of her as fearless. And no doubt she was in the way she looked at and analyzed the world. Being afraid of people she had to address publicly, on the other hand, was something I was familiar with and could empathize with.

And so I set off again. Like I had for Rosa Luxemburg and Hildegard von Bingen. Even traveling all the way to New York this time.

During my first trip there, I asked Pam Katz, with whom I'd written the screenplay for *Rosenstrasse*, if she could imagine a movie about Hannah Arendt. I was expecting a negative response, like my own initial one. But no—Pam was enthusiastic from the start; in fact, if it had been up to her, she would've started working on the project right away. Pam is Jewish and a New Yorker, so she has two important things in common with Arendt.

The next day, we drove to the Upper West Side to look at 370 Riverside Drive, where Hannah Arendt had last lived with her husband. I already knew the area, because Uwe Johnson, whose *Jahrestage* I had adapted for the screen, had also lived on Riverside for a while. Johnson had been friends with Hannah Arendt; the two of them even corresponded. But I didn't know that yet at the time. We took pictures of the building, entrance, and lobby. An initial approach. I need this sort of concrete image. In my imagination, right away, I pictured Hannah walking in and out of the entrance.

Even so, I couldn't quite believe that Pam was so readily willing to take on Hannah Arendt—that she didn't have to struggle through a forest of doubt first, as I had had to do. And so I suddenly found myself caught between two people pushing me to take the leap. Yet neither of them was a director. Their imaginations didn't have to transform a text into a living, moving picture. That's an enormous difference. Writing may not be easy, but as long as images remain in the imagination, anything is possible and imaginable.

A director's work begins the moment you have to turn images in your head into externally visible ones—and that's also where the agony begins.

To give you just one example. In the screenplay for *Marianne and Juliane*, I had written, carelessly and succinctly: "They climb Mount Etna." Just one, harmless-sounding sentence. And then the whole team, plus the actors, had to drag themselves up the mountain. It was especially tough for me because I was still a heavy smoker at the time, and the smell of sulfur was so intense I could hardly breathe. In the end, our gaffer had to push me from behind, which was pretty humiliating.

At the time, I cursed that one sentence in the screenplay. But most of the time it's a question of much more difficult transpositions. An author describes a certain atmosphere—between day and night, let's say, in the twilight of feelings or in a certain landscape. And then there you are, standing on the set, and that atmosphere just refuses to materialize. You're working against the clock, you're under pressure from your producer because every day of shooting is tremendously expensive, so you have no choice but to make compromises.

Hannah Arendt! It's easy to write: she is a thinker—or, she thinks. But how can you convincingly show that in a movie? And what was she, anyway?

Jerome Kohn wrote:

She is usually called a philosopher and often described as a political and moral philosopher. But I wonder. Was Socrates a philosopher? He was a thinker, to be sure, and a lover of wisdom, which is what philosopheia means in Greek. But do we know what wisdom is? We should not forget that Socrates insisted he knew nothing. Might that have been the reason the Delphic Oracle proclaimed him the wisest of all men? Hannah Arendt was a thinker with a need to understand. She said she could not live without trying to understand whatever happened, and the times she lived through were replete with events, many of them unprecedented, each of them difficult to understand in itself, and more difficult to understand collectively. Catastrophic events, one after the other, "cascading like a Niagara Falls of History," as Hannah Arendt put it.

Since the history of the twentieth century—and, with it, Hannah Arendt's life—was packed with events "like . . . Niagara Falls," where should we start describing her life? With her childhood in Königsberg? When she took part in Martin Heidegger's seminar—the master of thinking, as Arendt later called him? When she escaped from Germany in 1933, via Prague to France? With her exile in Paris, where she met Walter Benjamin and her future husband Heinrich Blücher? When the German armies invaded France and Hannah was sent to an internment camp? Or with her escape from there to Marseille and from Marseille via Lisbon to New York?

Perhaps you're familiar with the excellent film trilogy by Axel Corti, written by Georg Stefan Troller, that describes the fate of Vienna Jews who flee, via France, to the United States, where they are forced to live in extreme poverty at first. Hannah Arendt and Heinrich Blücher didn't have any money when they arrived in New York, either, and they didn't speak English. Like a much younger woman, Hannah Arendt had to find work as an au pair for a middle-class American family to learn the language. In 1941, when she was already thirty-five years old. Any one of these episodes could have been made into a riveting, dramatic film. So which one should we choose?

It quickly became clear to us that we didn't want to write a love story à la "Hannah and Marty," even though we undoubtedly would have found the money for it much faster. We were convinced that her husband Heinrich Blücher was the more important man in her life.

After Rosa Luxemburg and Hildegard von Bingen, I wasn't really in the mood for a so-called bio-pic. Moreover, it seemed like a leap in the dark to me, with no chance to linger, no time to think or reflect.

Luckily for me, I found out that Lotte Köhler, a colleague and friend of Hannah Arendt, was still alive and living in New York. She welcomed me warmly, but also with skepticism.

She couldn't imagine that a film could do justice to her friend, and she had just had an unpleasant experience with a writer to whom, years earlier, she had entrusted Martin Heidegger's letters to Arendt, when they were still unpublished. This writer had used the letters to cobble together a kitschy play that had infuriated Köhler. As a result, she was wary of me. It was only after seeing *Rosa Luxemburg* that she opened up to me more. She told me that Hannah Arendt had been a great admirer of Rosa Luxemburg, that she had even written an essay about her. In time, Lotte Köhler told us many anecdotes nowhere to be found in any of the biographies.

Köhler also put us in touch with Elisabeth Young Bruehl, Hannah Arendt's first biographer, who had studied with her. She had since become a psychoanalyst, which, by her own admission, would not have pleased Arendt. She, too, helped us—thanks in particular to her different, psychoanalytic point of view. She described Hannah's fixation on older men—Heidegger, Jaspers, and Blumenfeld, for example—as a search for her father, who had died much too early.

But it was Jerome Kohn who became—and has remained to this day—our key contact. These three people—Lotte Köhler, Elisabeth Young Bruehl, and Jerome— soon became as important and close to us as this "tribe" had been to Hannah Arendt. Every time I went to New York, we would meet for dinner, feeling a bit like romantic conspirators.

The last member of the "tribe" that we met was Hans Jonas's widow, Lore Jonas, in a senior-citizens home in Philadelphia. She gave us an unpublished letter her husband had written, in which he breaks off his friendship with Hannah after having read her articles in the *New Yorker*.

In the meantime, four years had passed, we had read almost all of Arendt's books and writings, and yet we still couldn't decide what period of her life to focus on and what scene to begin with. Finally, we had our eureka moment: we would concentrate on the Eichmann years. Reporting for the *New Yorker*, Hannah Arendt travels to Jerusalem to witness Adolf Eichmann's trial. This gave me a counterpart for her: a flesh-and-blood human being sitting in a glass box; not an abstract idea, but a man we could observe together, allowing us to participate in her thought process.

Hannah Arendt and Adolf Eichmann were both born in Germany—and even in the same year: 1906. But what diametrically opposed life stories! A German Nazi opportunist and a Jewish intellectual forced to flee Germany. The philosopher and the man who willingly abdicated his ability to think to "the Führer."

It was only when we hit upon this solution that my fear gradually faded and I became cautiously optimistic. It quickly became clear to me that in order to convincingly portray this meeting of two worlds I would have to use the original black-and-white footage from the Eichmann trial. Years earlier, before I had even the slightest idea that I'd be asked to make a movie about Hannah Arendt, I had seen a documentary, *The Specialist*, by Eyal Sivan, entirely about the Eichmann trial. I wanted to be sure that I could use this material. By this point, we had found a producer who was willing to go to bat for the film. She contacted Yad Vashem and managed to get us access to the footage we needed.

As had already been the case for Rosa Luxemburg and Hildegard von Bingen, letters were my main source for understanding both Arendt's political and private self. There was her correspondence with Karl Jaspers, who initially was supposed to play a part in the film; with Mary McCarthy, her American friend; and with Heidegger, though it is almost exclusively his letters that have survived. Hannah Arendt carefully collected and saved them in the drawer of her bedside table, while he seems to have been more inclined to get rid of hers—either because they weren't important enough to him or because he feared arousing his wife's jealousy. Arendt also exchanged letters with Kurt Blumenfeld, Hermann Broch, Gershom Scholem, and many others, which we were able to consult in the archives of the New School, where Hannah Arendt taught.

Since every person shows every other person a different side of his or her character, I find I'm best at bringing into focus a picture of a complex person from this kaleidoscope of impressions.

The more I read, the more Arendt became a friend to me. Lotte Köhler called her a "genius of friendship." And, in conclusion, I'd like to read an excerpt from one of her letters that confirms this. It is a reply to a letter from Gershom Scholem, who accused her of not loving her people: "You're quite right to say that I have no such love—and for two reasons. Firstly, I've never loved any people or collective in my life—not the Germans, French or Americans, nor the working class or anything else of that sort. The truth is that I love only my friends and am completely incapable of any other kind of love."

I could say the same of myself.

Thank you.

A Conversation with Margarethe von Trotta

Rem Berger / 2014

From *Double Exposure*, http://doubleexposurejournal.com/a-conversation-with -margarethe-von-trotta/, February 27, 2014. Reprinted by permission of Rem Berger.

Rem Berger: In an interview at the Goethe Institute about your new film *Hannah Arendt*, you compared the Nouvelle Vague to the New German Cinema. You said the Nouvelle Vague was a movement that mainly opposed conventions within cinema, whereas New German Cinema was more politically minded.

Margarethe von Trotta: Not all of my films are political. We were politically minded because we all came from the movement of '68 and because in our country the past was ignored. During the 1950s nobody spoke about National Socialism, nobody spoke about our past. In our school we had no information, and our parents wouldn't tell us about it either. It was all a big silence, but we still felt it. I tried to show that in *Marianne and Juliane* (1981). The original German title of the film is *Die Bleierne Zeit*, which means "The Leaden Times." It is derived from the poem "Der Gang Aufs Land" (The Walk in the Country) by Hölderlin. For me the title symbolizes the atmosphere in the fifties: not know anything, but feeling it.

RB: So regarding the scene in which the young Juliane is punished for saying she doesn't like the poem they're studying—something like that could have occured in real life? Would the teachers have reacted that severely?

MvT: Yes. Absolutely, because that line Juliane wants to speak about is from a poem by Brecht, and Brecht was a leftist who spoke about the Nazi past very clearly. The teacher only wants to discuss poets such as Rilke or Benn, who don't touch upon the past or history or politics. And therefore, when the truth finally came out and suddenly we had a picture of what happened—after seeing films of the Holocaust and so on—we were so angry and we were so destroyed, perhaps even more so than in our parents' generation. This is why we were all so angry and very politically minded.

The Nouvelle Vague didn't have this problem, on the other hand. They were invaded by Germany. They didn't attack us, we attacked them. Of course they also had something to hide: the fact that they had collaborated. In general, however, they were the victims and not the aggressors. So they only had to go up against the big studio films; all the films that were carefully produced within a studio, never outside on the street, and so that was their counterpart. It was also partly our counterpart, seeing as we didn't have the possibility financially to make big films in a studio. Because of this we learned from the Nouvelle Vague to go out into the street, to cast non-professional actors, and to just describe the life around us.

RB: You started your career as an actress and you made your way into directing in the seventies. Is directing something you always wanted to do, or did your ambitions change along the way?

MvT: I wanted to direct from the beginning! When I went to Paris to study in the early sixties I saw the films of Ingmar Bergman. That was for me the revelation of my life.

RB: Your film *Die Bleierne Zeit* has been compared to *Persona*. Is that a pertinent comparison?

MvT: Yes, but I didn't actually know *Persona* when I did the film. That's the strange thing: I was so involved in what Bergman was doing, that I made the film like he would have to a certain extent. But I didn't know *Persona*. It was only afterwards that many people made the comparison.

Bergman was my master, his work was a real cultural shock for me, and from that moment on I wanted to become a director. But as you know for women in the sixties it was unthinkable to become a director. You could become an actress, but not a director, so I started off as an actress. It wasn't like I had a plan to do that first and finally end up as a director. It was just an innocent and unconscious way to get into cinema. When the New German Cinema started, I soon met Volker Schlöndorff and I collaborated with him up until the point that I knew I could begin to direct.

RB: Was there something that changed with time, which allowed women to become directors?

MvT: Yes, there was change. In the mid-sixties there were some female directors already, but they mainly made documentaries. It was very difficult to get funding as a woman. This is much less the case today, but it still is difficult.

RB: Was there something that other films of the New German Cinema seemed to lack that you wanted to bring to the screen?

MvT: Yes, it was the woman's seeing into the world. We had other interests and other emotions than my male colleagues. But it was not pre-planned. I just wanted to make films, even without a political purpose. I didn't go into films to express my political views. I wanted to make films and sit in a dark room to see them and feel emotions. And seeing as we lived in a politically minded time, that came out in my films naturally. I started as an artist and not as a political activist.

RB: A recurring theme that has been picked up on in New German Cinema, is the portrayal of the protagonist as an outsider. I was wondering whether you would see this as a key element of the movement.

MvT: I don't think I ever reflected upon it. As a woman I was of course always an outsider; I was always in rebellion, and I had to rebel because nobody gave me what I wanted deliberately. You always needed to fight to get something, so for me it was definitely true.

Wim Wenders and Volker Schlöndorff were the only ones of us that went to film school. Schlöndorff went to film school here in Paris and also spent his assistant years here with Louis Malle, Jean Pierre Melville, and Alain Resnais. Fassbinder didn't go to film school, neither did Werner Herzog and nor did I.

My icon was Bergman, whereas Wim Wenders loved American films. Volker also wanted to go to America to make films, because that was the country of cinema. Fassbinder was a homosexual as well, so in a way even more of an outsider than we were. He also came from a very modest and uneducated family, so he educated himself. I was a woman who wanted to get into a profession that was normally only acceptable for men. That was my outsider position. And Herzog, well, he is from another planet, isn't he? He never did films in Germany; he always went out into the world. Herzog is now living in America. Wenders did his films inside Germany, but always with a longing for America, with a longing to go away. His road movies show that, seeing as the characters never stay in one place. He is constantly moving. And I myself went to Italy where I made three films and then came here to Paris, so I was stateless until my first marriage. We were all outsiders, and I guess that's why we ended up describing this state.

RB: So the theme of the outsider originated from the fact that you all identified yourselves with films or culture from outside of West Germany.

MvT: Yes, and we didn't have so much of that going on in Germany. If you look at the films that were made in West Germany in the fifties, they were nothing. They were just bad.

RB: Those so-called Heimat films from the 1950s were very escapist. Was it one of your aims to make your films anti-Heimat?

MvT: Not consciously. It's just that we didn't take those films seriously. My mother and I went to the cinema in the fifties when it was raining on Sundays and we had nothing else to do. It was just entertainment. We didn't take it seriously. So when I saw Ingmar Bergman's films I thought: "Ah! So that's what you can do with film! That is art!" For me, art was painting and music and theatre. I was very connected to art, my father was a painter, but film for me was no art, and only in France did I consider or discover it as a possibility of art.

RB: Sometimes I regret growing up in my generation, because film is just everywhere for me now. I don't think I ever had a moment like that, a moment in which I discovered film in that way.

MvT: When I went to the cinema in the early sixties here in Paris I could still buy one ticket and stay in the cinema for the whole afternoon, so you could watch the film three times. That was the only possibility to see certain things and look at them more precisely. Then video came out, which allowed you to fast forward, rewind, and so on and learn how they did it. You could really study it, but nevertheless, like Truffaut said, it helps you only if you saw the film first on the big screen. Then you have the first impact, the first impression, and it stays with you. What's so wonderful about going to the cinema is that it's like you're in your own dream. It's almost as if you are in your bed in the dark.

My two masters are Bergman and Hitchcock, and Hitchcock is the perfect dream director. When you think about your own dreams, you don't remember everything. And with a film of Hitchcock, you can see it even three times, you don't really remember what you've seen. You're very impressed the moment you are there, but when you look back it's really like remembering a horror dream; for Hitchcock it's always horror.

RB: You come away from a film and you have this impression, this atmosphere, but you only may remember a few sequences.

MvT: But these few sequences, they really stay with you long after you've seen the film. For instance, the first Bergman film I saw was *The Seventh Seal*, which starts with a shot of the sky, a very dramatic sky, and in the sky there's a black bird. I was only able to see the film once, and that was in 1961! Then in 2008 I did a film about Hildegard von Bingen, the medieval nun. So, like *The Seventh Seal* it is a film about the medieval times. I started to write my script, and at the beginning of the film I wrote about a dramatic sky with a black bird in it. I then held a lecture about Bergman at the embassy of Sweden in Berlin; they invited me to speak about him because I had also known him personally by then. When they asked me which film I wanted to show I said *The Seventh Seal*, because that was the film that had started everything for me. And when I saw the film again I realized where the idea of the dramatic sky had come from! But I hadn't remembered it at all: it was in my unconscious mind. I changed the script immediately, so now my film doesn't start like this. This is how images can stay with you. Your mind is like a big pool into which you deposit the images you see. You put them there, and when you write, ideas come out of it.

RB: So, even when you don't know that you've remembered sequences from films ages ago, they still pop into your head. That's one of the beautiful things about cinema. The film becomes almost like a time capsule for who you were at the time you made it, because you preserve all the ideas you had at the time that you didn't even mean to put into the film.

MvT: Absolutely. For example, I recently interpreted the beginning of my film, *Rosa Luxemburg*. It starts with an image for the sky and a wall on which two soldiers are walking in opposite directions. Then we pan far down and in the depths walks Rosa with a black raven walking behind her. When I did it at the time, it was just because I liked it that way. It was only afterwards that I found a real interpretation: Rosa is down in the depths and she wants to free and to liberate mankind. There in the sky is the symbol of freedom and liberty. She who wants to become free and free others walks down there. All of a sudden the shot has a meaning that I never intended.

That's what's so wonderful about filmmaking and of any form of art: that you have a feeling about something, and the meaning comes afterwards. You just have to trust your intuitions.

RB: When Thomas Elsaesser talks about your films, he says that they, and especially *The German Sisters*, stand out because you structure the films in such a way that identification with the main characters becomes a very important element. Seeing as your films are often about people who have opinions that aren't favored in the society in which they live, the films are actually made with the aim of having the audience sympathize with characters that they perhaps wouldn't understand in real life.

MvT: Yes. I've now made *Hannah Arendt*, and she says one line which has been mine from the beginning, and it is, "I want to understand." That's my philosophy of filmmaking. I don't want to judge or to criticize, I want to understand. And I want to understand people who are maybe not so understandable for others, people who are immediately criticized or victimized like Hannah Arendt. And people are always attacked by others, because not everyone has this longing to understand.

RB: Hannah Arendt also underlines the importance of our capacity to think. We question morality, and the fact that we do that already makes it important. Like

Hannah Arendt said, one of the fundamental things we can do is to question ourselves.

MvT: Absolutely, and you can make your own opinion. You can look at the world and judge yourself in relation to it. Don't give up on this capacity! This wonderful possibility of an ideology. And now, with all this media and all these opinions going around, so many people are giving up their own capacity to think. They let others do it for them.

RB: Technology often ensures that you don't have to think. It's like what is said in *Hannah Arendt*: "thinking is a lonely business."

MvT: But it's also satisfactory. It could also be a passion to think for yourself. Although it can be a lot of work, it's something wonderful!

RB: In *Nation and Identity* Inga Scharf argues that New German Cinema was built around the showing of discontentment with society—like you said, showing the emptiness of the 1950s because of the neglect of the past—and that the movement became too stuck in doing so. The movement became too focused on expressing their discontent as opposed to suggesting alternatives, and this could be a reason why the movement came to an end somewhere near the end of the eighties.

MvT: Maybe there's some truth in that, because throughout the seventies and the beginning of the eighties we had a hope to change society. We were all leftist and we wanted to make a real democracy. It was very utopian in a way. We were also a little bit naïve. And then in the middle of the eighties this hope to change the world declined. Perhaps every movement starts very strong in the beginning and ends with a certain tiredness.

We originally made an impact because we were a big group. There were so many all of a sudden and they all did very different films. We did very different films but we were all together. It was like a pressure group coming up all together, making films all together in one moment. And so the world looked at us.

By the mid-eighties, we were no longer this group, this force, because Fassbinder died in '82, Wim went to America, and Schlöndorff also wanted to go away. We all wanted to leave Germany and in 1988 I went to Italy. It felt like something was over and you can't force yourself to stay with it. Perhaps it's a natural development.

RB: In the interview at the Goethe Institute you compare Rosa Luxemburg to Hannah Arendt. I think you said something along the lines of: "I took, in my eyes, the most important woman of the first half of the twentieth century and now the most important woman of the second half."

MvT: Those are explanations you give to it afterwards. In the moment I didn't choose a person because I thought she was the most important person of that time. But afterwards we give all these intellectual explanations to it.

RB: This is actually one of the reasons I really wanted to speak to you. It's because I realize I am writing about something which is quite a personal matter, seeing as you were expressing how it was to live in West Germany at the time. I was hoping you could further explicate your notion of national identity.

MvT: For me it is very easy to explain: firstly I'm a filmmaker and an artist. For me film is a passion and the only way to receive the world, to look at the world and then put it into images. And on top of that I'm living in a certain time, a certain epoch, and I'm looking outside and I see what's happening. And that then comes into my films. But it's not on purpose. I don't say: "Now I have to do a film about Germany in the eighties." It comes because I'm living in a certain moment and I'm living with open eyes. And that's it! It comes naturally.

RB: And that's a part of being a good artist. I once read a quote by Michael Haneke in which he said something along the lines of: "Every time I open a film book, I read about what I supposedly meant to do with my films, but didn't at all." It's actually quite interesting that the conclusion we've reached here is that so much of the filmmaking process is unconscious.

MvT: Yes, and it has to be. The importance of art is that you [leave] such space for the unconscious to come in. That is art! Ask a painter why he chose the color blue in his painting. He chose it because he feels that he has to do it in this very moment. Then afterwards you can say that blue means coldness or this or that, but if he would do this in the moment it would be terrible. It's a reduction of everything if you do it before. Marco Bellocchio, for instance, made wonderful films. And at a certain moment he met a psychoanalyst who became very important in his life, he did everything with him and consulted him when he made films and so on, and then all of a sudden he did films in which he would show water, because water meant something, he would show fire, because fire meant something, you know, in Freudian symbolism. And then they had no meaning anymore. It was just all applied. Symbols were applied, and now that he's separated from this guy, he makes good films again. For me that was the proof that you don't have to know the meaning beforehand to make a meaningful work of art.

RB: Are there things that you were trying to express, consciously or unconsciously, back in the seventies and eighties that are still relevant today?

MvT: I never look my films up again, only when I am forced to do it, but people tell me that *Die Bleierne Zeit* is still relevant today. I also think, and again this is an interpretation that came after I made it, the film is not only about German sisters, but also about two different attitudes towards the German politics in the moment I made it; it was also about sisters and their differences in characters.

RB: Which is perhaps a timeless thing.

MvT: Yeah, it's like the Greek tragedy of Ismene and Antigone, which also revolves around the relationship between a more docile and rebellious sister. It is a timeless dynamic.

RB: I was wondering about *Die Bleierne Zeit*: in one of the flashbacks of the sisters, like the ones we were talking about, Juliane is reading a book by Jean-Paul Sartre. Was that a deliberate reference to existentialism?

MvT: Yes, she is reading it because her father is a pastor, a protestant priest, and her sister will go to Africa to save the world, to save the people who are ill, whereas she is reading a treatise on existentialism. And that has also to do with me, because that was a time in which I was in Paris and I read Sartre and Beauvoir.

RB: Do you still believe in his philosophy?

MvT: No, now I'm much more on the side of Camus. When I was studying here I also liked Camus. It was a sort of existentialism we didn't have in Germany so it was very attractive to us.

RB: Once again this shows your identification with something outside of Germany.

There's one quote I read from you in which you talk about how a hierarchial way of thinking inspires the separation between one's personal and private life, whereas these should go hand in hand. Also, characters in your films combine their public and private life, because they speak openly about their private thoughts.

MvT: Yes, that was also a feminist statement in the seventies or the early eighties, that the private is also political. They are intertwined. You have to look to how people behave in their private life and not only how they behave in public.

I tried to do that in *Rosa Luxemburg*. She was always complaining that her comrades, the social democratic comrades, said one thing in public and did just the opposite in their private lives. As women we so often had the feeling that men in public said, "Yes, we have to do something for women!," and then when you look at how they treat their own wives at home, it is just the opposite. So, that was the rebellion of our feminist part of the seventies.

"Everybody Is a Kaleidoscope": An Interview with Margarethe von Trotta

Monika Raesch / 2015

Phone interview conducted on August 18, 2015. Reprinted by permission of Monika Raesch.

Monika Raesch: The two topics I want to talk about in more depth in this interview is authorship (das Autorenkino) as it has surfaced in so many of your interviews over the decades starting in the eighties; and the other topic is the topic of film adaptation since so many of your works are adapted or based on novels, or inspired by real-life situations. There has not really been a discourse that I could find on your process of adapting since you were writing screenplays.

Margarethe von Trotta: In terms of adaptation, I never adapted . . . it was just only one for television. That's my ex-husband Volker Schlöndorff; he always adapted novels into cinema print, but practically all my films are originals. Only what I'm doing in biography like with the new project . . . then I have to base it off the life and the writings and the letters of this person.

MR: So, how do you approach an original text—whether that is the facts of Rosa Luxemburg's life when you decide to adapt something like that into a film? What steps do you take?

MvT: It's really very, very complicated how to approach . . . And it is always in a different way, but mainly when I make a film about these persons in history or in literature or philosophy, my main source are letters, personal correspondences the person has had in their lifetime. Because I think you can feel a person much better from the inside than from the outside. From inside . . . the letter, because with every person you are corresponding [with] you have a special tone. It depends on the person you are addressing. If you have different correspondences or persons with whom you are corresponding . . . there are many different aspects. It's a little bit like a kaleidoscope . . . in the end you feel the person from the inside.

Also, you are sure you have the [curriculum] vitae and if it's possible you also interview people who knew the character, the person you are describing. In the case of Hannah Arendt, we still had three or four people we could ask. One was her very good friend in New York, Dr. Köhler; she was still alive. And her personal assistant and student, Christian Bruehl. These two are already dead now, but her last assistant—he is still alive. These three persons helped us a lot to understand [Hannah Arendt's] being or her character.

MR: Given that you spoke about Rosa Luxemburg and given that you take such careful consideration, do you read any criticism from critics afterwards about the way you adapted a person? Or do you purposefully stay away from it?

MvT: It depends, because sometimes film critics are not so well informed about people . . . and that happened with both Rosa Luxemburg and Hannah Arendt. These people [the critics] have nothing to do with film, so they are attacking you because you are not precise enough about the historical events. Therefore, I also wrote the "History in Film" [lecture], because history in film is not a documentary.

Film is not a documentary, so you have the right and permission to inject your own imagination and you even have to because you can't find every scene in books. You have to invent . . . but it must only go in the direction of truth and of the character itself. You cannot invent freely. Now, many historic writers covering the medieval Hildegard von Bingen . . . there are books about her now and they are terrible, because they are total inventions. And then it becomes "kitsch" [that is, works of inferior quality that are cheap and imitative]. If you go with the truth and with the character, then you can do that.

MR: In general, how do you select material for a film? For instance, for the WDR when you created *Dunkle Tage/Dark Days*, and while it is fictional, you selected a true event and decided to use realistic actions.

MvT: It's a story I invented, but I invented it on the basis of many, many books I read on alcoholism and people who are addicted to alcohol. I spoke with people. I am not addicted to alcohol and nobody in my family is either, so I didn't have an example to look at. But I read so many things . . . I educated myself this way. But the film is not based on a special story. It is based on a story I invented.

MR: How do you select a topic or theme for a film? Does material choose you? Do you select material?

MvT: That is so complex and so different . . . with every film it's a different story. I can't tell you in general but I can tell you for each film individually how I chose it or how it came up to me. When I wrote for *Rosa Luxemburg* and also for *Rosenstrasse*, they are themes coming to you from the outside. And they are proposed to you or they are given as an idea to you, and in the first instance you say: "no, no, I am not capable of that." You don't trust yourself, you are not confident enough to think that you are on the level of the person you have to describe. You say "no, no, no." And then, it starts to grow in your mind, and when something is put in your mind like a theme, then it starts to grow and then you can't refuse it anymore. And then you start the research. But there are other themes, like for my second film, *The Second Awakening of Christa Klages*, that are just coming out of myself. Sitting in front of a white page, and I start to write. It's like the flow of unconscious that is coming out from you. You become conscious of it at that moment, but it comes from your unconscious.

MR: How much do you then feel a screenwriter's personal life impacts what you are writing in the end?

MvT: I think that is always very, very important. You are choosing or describing sort of your own life in another person, or it comes in without you even knowing it. But you are choosing . . . For instance, with *Rosa Luxemburg*, there would be so many different ways to approach the person, and you are choosing of that [person's] life what your interest is. It's not a search of identity, but sort of kinship in emotion and in thinking.

MR: Given what you just said about feeling a relation with the person you are creating, can screenwriting be collaborative? For example, you wrote *The Promise* with Peter Schneider. Does it make it harder to create characters that not only you can relate to but you also have to share them with somebody else?

MvT: It depends. With Peter Schneider, that was a project called "The Wall." An Italian producer came up to me and said "Margarethe, you have to make a film about these wall years." And I said, "Oh, I am not capable because I did not live all this time in Berlin. There must be somebody who knows everything about this time, having been in Berlin." And so Peter Schneider, a friend of ours, and I asked him whether he would be interested in writing a script. The idea [of the story] that the couple was separated by the wall, that was his idea. If I would have written it myself [Margarethe begins to laugh as she speaks], it would have probably been two sisters or two girlfriends [more laughter] being separated. His idea of the couple, that came from him, and I had to follow him.

MR: And this collaboration worked harmoniously for the most part?

MvT: We worked sitting together and we were speaking, and then he wrote it down. We were sitting in front of a computer, and he wrote it down. I was not so much involved in writing myself. He is the writer. I am also a writer, but I am only a scriptwriter. He is a novelist. Another film I did in Italy, *Love and Fear*, I wrote together with an Italian writer, Dacia Maraini, and that was the same, because it was written for an Italian producer, and we had to write it in Italian. We discussed and spoke about everything, and then she wrote it down. But normally when I am alone, I sit in front of the computer.

Sometimes I follow facts or what I know about an event or a person or a time, a particular story of a given time, or I just wait for what comes up. And sometimes . . . For instance, right now I am writing a script . . . Sometimes I am starting, I have to read a lot about these people, and then I start with one sentence. And one sentence leads me to others through the whole scene. I just have to start and then it comes up automatically out of myself.

MR: What do you think is the role of the screenwriter in relation to the final product, which is unique in your case as most of the time you are directing the final product as well?

MvT: When you are a scriptwriter, then comes in the director, so he has to be very careful with the text. Mainly, in American classic filmmaking you really have to respect the script and and the words a lot. When I am the director and I wrote the script as well, I am free to say the opposite during the shooting from what I wrote in the script. I am not responsible to nobody, but to myself.

MR: Does it happen often that you change your mind on the set?

MvT: Yes, even when we are reading with the actors, an actor may say "I can't say that; it's not my style of dialogue, of talk." Then I try to find something else.

MR: Lots of critics have said that you create open endings [in your films], that that has become a signature of yours. Why do you tend to create the endings that you tend to create; whether they are open endings is up for debate. Is there something that you are trying to achieve? How do you know what the ending is for a story?

MvT: It depends on the story. Not all my work has open endings. When a film is ending with the death of somebody, like *Rosa Luxemburg*, she is thrown in the Landwehrkanal, it's the perfect ending [for that story], because it's also the real ending of her life and not just of the story. On the other hand, I like to leave things open for the storytelling of the audience. Alexander Kluge is another German director from the generation of New German Cinema. He once said: "Every film is completed in the mind of the spectator."

MR: This is very similar to Abbas Kiarostami [Iranian director]; he called it 'the unfinished cinema.'

MvT: I like that. Every spectator can compose or invent his or her own ending.

MR: This brings me to the next topic, authorship cinema. Since we just spoke about endings from a writing perspective, critics have noted other signatures of your films as recurrent actresses, cinematographer, assistant. How important is it for you with the same people over consecutive films?

MvT: I had very few directors of photography in my life. In Italy, I did three films and I had three different directors [of photography]. But in the beginning, in Germany, I always worked with Franz Rath. From a certain point onwards I changed to Axel Block, and I did several films with him. I only had two or three other DOPs [directors of photography] in my life. It's the same with actors. I did seven films with Barbara Sukowa and now three films with Katja Riehman. If the characters are fitting with these actresses or actors, then I am faithful. If we work well together, then I am faithful, because with every film you do together, you go deeper and deeper into what you want to do and want to express. With Barbara, for instance, we know each other so well, we only need to look at each other and we know immediately what we want . . . what Barbara wants to say and what I want to say. We don't even need words anymore. And we are preparing ourselves before we are shooting. For instance, she reads all the texts I read for writing [the script]. She reads the same things for acting, and then we speak about them. Sometimes she even finds a text that I didn't find and she shows it to me . . . a text of Rosa Luxemburg, for example. Hers was a better one than the one I had chosen, so we took hers. We are really a working team. Not only as actress and director, but also as intellectuals.

MR: Do you have the same sort of relationship in terms of cinematography with your DOP? That you are a similar working team, just not on the topic of how to develop the character but on the topic of how to shoot the scene?

MvT: Yes, that's the way we are. With the German director of photography we are preparing very well, mainly with Franz Rath; we sit down and we really do a decoupage. We talk about every shot. With Axel Block we sometimes speak before, but then we are also open to change on the set. We are speaking together about how to do the film. In Italy, where I did three films, it was totally different, because there you had the DOP who is only responsible for the lighting and then you have the operator who has to operate the camera. In Germany, this person is one, making lighting and operating the camera. So you can talk with the [German] DOP about everything. In Italy, they just wanted me to say "camera here" and "this movement here" and so on. They only followed what I was saying. That was very new to me and I felt a little bit alone, being accustomed to having a partner.

MR: Given what you just said about preferring to work in teams, and given that we are also talking about authorship cinema, who or what, in your opinion, is the author of the final product?

MvT: I think it is the director. You have to have collaborators who are giving you their ideas. My collaborators are very, very close to me, but I always am the last one to say "yes" or "no," to make the decision.

MR: What is your opinion on "la politique des auteurs"? Do you see merit in it from your perspective as a filmmaker? Do you have an uneasy relationship of always being judged by your signatures? Or you don't mind?

MvT: I cannot judge the others [such as critics]. I can just tell [them] what I am doing. You are not capable to do everything; you have to take your own road. The films you make depend on yourself, your character, your emotions, and your own perspective of looking at the world. And even if you would like to be somebody else, "I would like to do a film in another way," that does not work. I always return to my own road . . .

MR: . . . regardless of what the critics are saying.

MvT: Yes. My films always have something to do with me.

MR: For instance, it has been argued that one of the reasons you moved to Rome in 1988 was Germany's increasingly negative attitude towards auteur cinema at the time. When you read things like that about yourself do you have a reaction?

MvT: [laughing] "What do they [the journalists] know?"

MR: What signatures, if any, would you like to be known for, that you feel represent your work?

MvT: [pondering for a moment] I dislike the [existing] cliché "she only creates movies about women . . . why doesn't she make moves about men." I dislike clichés. I don't like those. One woman in Italy wrote a book about me. She analyzed my films so deeply, including literature, music, biology. She studied my work from a variety of viewpoints that I also find interesting in my day-to-day life. Every person is a kaleidoscope of characteristics, talents, interests, emotions. Everybody is so many possible persons in one. I would like [critics and scholars] to take that approach. I am not only a person who writes about women, a person who is always political . . . All these labels that I have been given . . . One has to look at the depth of a person. My films are a representation of me. One older actress who worked on two of my films said to me: "Your films are like icebergs. We only see a little peak of the iceberg. The main portion is under the water, out of sight." And this is what so many critics don't see. They are not interested to look further.

MR: I wonder whether it is due to the publications the critics write for and they have to cater to that. With limited word count per article, they cannot reach much depth. In those publications, you will find sentences such as a list of female auteurs that include Sofia Coppola, Kathryn Bigelow, Margarethe von Trotta, to argue that all these filmmakers are all women, all auteurs. Does that hold meaning to you, that you have reached the status of an auteur?

MvT: I don't like labels in general. I am always against them. I think one must have the right to be looked at in a new way every time [one makes a new film]. Reviewers need natural curiosity. Often, I feel that many critics are not really curious.

MR: You had given the comparison between Italian and German working experiences on a film. From your experience, in terms of creating films financed by different countries but also for different outlets, such as film and television work, how much impact does a studio have on a project?

MvT: I never worked with very important studios or very important producers. My producers are very often my friends. I don't have to defend myself much to them.

MR: Meaning you have more freedom?

MvT: Yes. I have freedom up to a certain point, but if you have no money . . . You only have freedom within the constraints of your budget, and that can be very limiting.

MR: Given that you are working with friends, has your work ever been impacted in such a way that you felt a conflict with your own vision and what you were forced to produce?

MvT: [ponders for a while] No.

MR: Why do you think that is?

MvT: Because I am not supposed to make films that are highly financially successful. If you are making films with a big budget, then you have to have success at the box office.

MR: Since you have made movies for several decades, has funding changed over the years?

MvT: Some of the films I made in the 1980s, I wouldn't be able to create today; I would not get money for them. They are very personal films. It has become more difficult to get money.

MR: Why is that? Is there an increased emphasis in profitability?

MvT: There are many more filmmakers in Germany. With the film schools, you have many new directors, and they all want to make films. In Germany, we are currently making too many films. They don't even make it to the cinema, or they are only running for one week or so. There is no chance to make a film grow in the cinema. When you don't make it in the first weekend or the second, the cinemas are throwing you out. There are so many films waiting for release. Cinemas can do what they want.

MR: So the power lies with the exhibitors.

MvT: The exhibitors.

MR: What do you think about services such as Netflix—online streaming, as opposed to trying to get it into the cinema?

MvT: Perhaps for younger people it's paradise. For me, I am not a fan of it. I would like for people to go into the darkened room of the cinema, sit down, and be transported into another world. That was my first experience with film and that is what I am always reaching for again. When you sit in the cinema in the dark, your mind is open to something else and that is what I was longing for when I went to the cinema at the beginning and I am still longing for that.

MR: What do you feel is the role of cinema in society?

MvT: You can do so many things. With new techniques, possibilities have emerged that you could not do in the past. But if you look at the German filmmakers from the twenties, Fritz Lang, Friedrich Murnau . . . they invented things that were really art and very suggestive, and now it's sometimes . . . it's only to "use it." It has nothing to do with the real research of meaning [in a film, a story]. I would like to touch people deeply; today it is mostly about aggression that you use techniques first. For instance, I wanted to see the latest *Mission Impossible.* I have only seen one before; and now the new one was released. You have the feeling that when you saw one, you have seen them all. Yes, they have new gadgets and techniques, but the main theme is always the same. And it has gotten more and more aggressive. I watched it in a cinema in Paris, a large cinema. They have all these trailers before the film begins—and it's all about aggression. You are in a way so tired and so exhausted by the time the actual film is starting already from the aggressive images in the trailers. When you look at movies from the past, like *Ben-Hur,* where they had so many tricks, and they were good; you could feel them. But now . . .

MR: Maybe this is where current directors should return to the first days of cinema where the trailers ran after the movie so you could just leave.

MvT: Yes, that is true. Now, you have already watched half an hour of trailers by the time the main film begins.

MR: Given your history as an actress, I know your goal had always been to be a director but at the time that was an impossibility, so you started acting instead. Alfred Hitchcock always made his cameo appearances. Why did you decide once you became a director to no longer act and also take parts in your own films?

MvT: From the beginning, I wanted to be a director, to make films myself. In the early sixties, you couldn't even imagine that a woman could do that. I didn't know how to step in. Becoming an actress was like an unconscious detour to enter the world of the film industry. When the New German Cinema started, I tried to enter into the milieu as an actress. When I had made several films and had met Volker Schlöndorff, we did films together. Little by little I learnt by observing. Eventually, the time arrived to dare a female director. I tried . . .

To be an actress was never my final wish. The final wish was to direct films myself, and that's why I have never acted again. I don't feel the need to act anymore. It helps that I was an actress; it helps a lot when working with actors now as a director. I don't blame the time period that I could only be actress. I benefit from it now.

MR: I want to double-check something. You just said "blame"—would it be better to use the word "regret" in the context?

MvT: Absolutely; yes, please.

MR: Given that this is an interview that is going to be published in a book, my final question on the topic of authorship and how others write about you is: do you read the biographies or texts that are written about you? Why or why not?

MvT: I read them if you ask me to look it up for questioning, if there is an error in a text, for example. Otherwise, I don't read them. I am bored with them. It's boring for me to read about myself. I read biographies of other people.

Additional Resources

Books

(in English)

Hehr, Renate. *Margarethe von Trotta: filmmaking as liberation*. Stuttgart: Ed. Axel Menges, 2000.

Levitin, Jacqueline. *Wolmen Filmmakers: Refocusing*. Florence: Taylor and Francis, 2012.

Linville, Susan E. *Feminism, Film, Fascism: Women's Auto/biographical Film in Postwar Germany*. Austin: University of Texas Press, 1998.

(in other languages)

Belser, Lorenz. *Rainer Werner Fassbinder, Margarethe von Trotta, Michelangelo Antonioni*. Zürich: Filmstellen VSETH/VSU, 1991.

De Miro d'Ajeta, Ester Carla. *Margarethe von Trotta: l'identità divisa*. Genova: Le Mani, 1999.

Fischetti, Renate. *Das neue Kino: acht Porträts von deutschen Regisseurinnen : Helke Sander, Claudia von Alemann, Ula Stöckl, Helma Sanders-Brahms, Margarethe von Trotta, Jutta Brückner, Ulrike Ottinger, Doris Dörrie*. Frankfurt am Main: Tende, 1992.

Schiavo, Maria. *Margarethe von Trotta : ovvero l'onore ritrovato*. Torino: A.I.A.C.E., 1985.

Wiebel, Martin. *Mutmassungen über Gesine : Uwe Johnsons 'Jahrestage' in der Verfilmung von Margarethe von Trotta*. Frankfurt: Suhrkamp, 2000.

Wydra, Thilo. *Margarethe von Trotta: Filmen, um zu überleben*. Berlin: Henschel, 2000.

———. *Rosenstrasse: ein Film von Margarethe von Trotta: die Geschichte, die Hintergründe, die Regisseurin*. Berlin: Nicolai, 2003.

Yang, Hui. *Auf dem Weg zur Emanzipation : Studie der Filme von Margarethe von Trotta unter frauenspezifischer Perspektive*. Frankfurt am Man: P. Lang, 2003.

Journal Articles and Book Chapters

(in English)

Coates, Paul. "Elective affinities and family resemblances: For Margarethe von Trotta." In *The Gorgon's Gaze: German Cinema, Expressionism, and the Image of Horror*, 193–228. Cambridge: Cambridge University Press, 1991.

Cormican, Muriel. "The Demands of Holocaust Representation: Formal Considerations in Margarethe von Trotta's *Rosenstraße*." *German Quarterly* 87, no. 4 (October 2014): 440–58.

Donougho, Martin. "Margarethe von Trotta: gynemagoguery and the dilemmas of a filmmaker." *Literature/Film Quarterly* 17, no. 3 (July 1989): 149–60.

Downey, Mike. "German Stories." *Cinema Papers*, no. 80 (August 1, 1990): 24–26.

Grobbel, Michaela. "The "Mischling" as a Trope for a New German-Jewish Identity? The Figure of the Girl in Ilse Aichinger's *Die grössere Hoffnung* and Margarethe von Trotta's *Rosenstrasse*." *Pacific Coast Philology* 44, no. 1 (January 1, 2009): 70–92.

Johnston, Sheila. "Margarethe von Trotta." In *Talking Films*. London: Fourth Estate Limited, 1991.

Kuttenberg, Eva. "The Hidden Face of Narcissus: Suicide as Poetic Speech in Margarethe von Trotta's Early Films." *Women in German Yearbook* 20 (January 1, 2004): 122–44.

Mccormick, Richard W. "Cinematic Form, History, and Gender in Margarethe von Trotta's Rosa Luxemburg." *Seminar: A Journal of Germanic Studies* 32, no. 1 (February 1996): 30–43.

Moeller, Hans-Bernhard. "The Films of Margarethe von Trotta: Domination, Violence, Solidarity, and Social Criticism. *Women in German Yearbook*, no. 2 (January 1, 1986): 129.

———."West German women's cinema: the case of Margarethe von Trotta." *Film Criticism* 9, no. 2 (Winter 1984–1985): 51–66.

Parkinson, Anna M. "Neo-feminist Mutterfilm? The Emotional Politics of Margarethe von Trotta's *Rosenstrasse*." In *The Collapse of the Conventional: German Film and Its Politics at the Turn of the Twenty-First Century*, edited by Jaimey Fisher and Brad Prager. Detroit: Wayne State University Press, 2010.

Robertson, Judith. "Teaching in Your Dreams: Screen-play Pedagogy and Margarethe von Trotta's *The Second Awakening of Christa Klages*." *Canadian Journal of Film Studies* 13, no. 2 (Fall 2004): 74–92.

Rosenberg, Joel. "Into the Woods: Eichmann, Heidegger, and Margarethe von Trotta's *Hannah Arendt*." *Jewish Film & New Media* 2, no. 2 (October 1, 2014): 201–16.

Scribner, Charity. "The Stammheim Complex in *Marianne and Juliane*." In *After the Red Army Faction: Gender, Culture and Militancy*. New York: Columbia University Press, 2014.

Sjöholm, Cecilia. "Margarethe von Trotta: Leviathan in Germany." In *Cinematic Thinking: Philosophical Approaches to the New Cinema*, edited by James Phillips. Stanford: Stanford University Press, 2008.

Steinberg, Michael. "Seeing Hearing Thinking: Introducing the differences Dossier von Margarethe von Trotta." *Differences* 26, no. 2 (2015): 61.

Von Trotta, Margarethe, and Bruno Ramirez. "Margarethe Von Trotta." In *Inside the Historical Film*, 190–201. McGill-Queen's University Press, 2014. http://www.jstor.org/stable/j. ctt7zto8r.14.

Winkle, Sally. "Margarethe von Trotta's *Rosenstrasse*: 'Feminist Re-Visions' of a Historical Controversy." In *A Companion to German Cinema*. UK: John Wiley &Sons, Inc., 2012.

(in other languages)

Alessio, Tommasoli. "The Dialogue Between Cinema and Philosophy: *Hannah Arendt* by Margarethe von Trotta." *Journal of Literature and Art Studies* 6, no. 4 (March 31, 2016).

Babich, Babette. "Thinking on Film: Jaspers, Scholem, and Thinking in Margarethe von Trotta's *Hannah Arendt*." *German Politics and Society* 34, no. 1 (Spring 2016): 77–92.

Dąbrowska, Diana. "Margarethe von Trotta: prywatne jest polityczne." *Kino* 50, no. 578, August 2015): 7–10.

Ebbecke-Nohlen, Andre, and Dieter Nohlen. "Hannah Arendt. Sus ideas cambian el mundo. Una película de Margarethe von Trotta." *Desafíos*, no. 1 (2015): 209–28.

Grunert, Andrea. "Trois soeurs de Margarethe von Trotta: 'On n'existe que si on est aimé.'" *CinémAction*, no. 146 (March 2013): 145–53.

Helman, Alicja. "Margarethe von Trotta." *Filmkultura* 21, no. 8 (August 1985): 3–11.

Henau, Gorik. "Hannah Arendt: Interview met Margarethe von Trotta." *Filmmagie*, no. 635 (May–June 2013): 39–40.

Hwang Junghyun. "'1989 in the Shadow of 1945': The Berlin Republic and Margarethe von Trotta's *The Promise*." 문학과영상 제11권 3호, 2010, 953–74.

Iarussi, Oscar. "Margarethe von Trotta." *Belfagor* 39 (January 1, 1984): 283.

Köhler, Margret. "Unsichtbare Wunden." *Film-dienst* 68, no. 9 (April 2015): 22–23.

Martin, Michel, and Maurice Elia. "Margarethe von Trotta toujours présente." *Séquences*, no. 187 (November–December 1996): 27–32.

Schneider, Roland. "Margarethe von Trotta: la longue marche vers l'émancipation." *CinémAction*, no. 28 (April 1984): 76–79.

Von Trotta, Margarethe, and Christel Buschmann. "Gespräch zwischen Margarethe von Trotta und Christel Buschmann." *Frauen und Film*, no. 8 (June 1, 1976): 29–33.

Video Resources

Acker, Ally. *Foreign Directors on Directing*. Reel Women Media, 2006.

———. *Screenwriters on Screenwriting*. Reel Women Media, 2009.

———. *The HerStory*. Reel Women Media, 2006.

Buschka, Peter. "Die Neugier immer weiter treiben—die filmische Befreiung der Margarethe von Trotta." *Regisseure des Neuen Deutschen Films-Collectors edition*. Kick Film GmbH, 1996.

Schlicht, Burghard. *Margarethe von Trotta—Mit Herz und Verstand*. 2006.

Index

Printed in the United States
By Bookmasters